Yolisa Qunta

writing what we like

A New Generation Speaks

TAFELBERG

Tafelberg
An imprint of NB Publishers, a Division of Media24 Boeke (Pty) Ltd
40 Heerengracht, Cape Town
www.tafelberg.com
Copyright in editing © Yolisa Qunta (2016)
Copyright contributions © Individual contributors

Cover design: Simon Richardson
Book design: Nazli Jacobs
Editing: Angela Voges
Proofreading: Sean Fraser

Printed by *paarlmedia*, a division of Novus Holdings
First edition, first impression 2016

ISBN: 978-0-624-07180-8
Epub: 978-0-624-07181-5
Mobi: 978-0-624-07182-2

This book is dedicated to the memory of Vuyisa Cebani Qunta, the first person to show me what unconditional love felt like. My father used to look at me like I was magic: made of spun gold and fairy dust. No matter how many mistakes I made, his unwavering belief in me gave me the strength to get back up and try again. I will be forever grateful that I lived long enough to see myself the same way his benevolent and all-forgiving gaze did. *Lala ngoxolo maMbongwe.*

Contents

Introduction

I grew up in the age before the internet and the widespread use of computers, so I have always turned to the printed book for information and knowledge. Even in this era of Google searches and online news agencies, I tend to fall back to the printed word for an accurate description of events in the present and the past.

The struggle to free South Africa was a long and well-documented one. Books, movies, songs, poems and paintings illustrate the hardships of living under colonialism and apartheid, and record the tremendous sacrifices made by those who fought to overthrow the system.

However, since 1994 very little has been written about life in this brave new world. I am surprised by the small offering of first-person accounts by the older generation, who have lived through apartheid, and the younger generation, who are seeing the changes for which their parents fought so hard becoming reality.

As the first generation to reach adulthood in a democratic South Africa, my peers and I are witnessing transformation and progress first hand. I feel strongly that we are duty-bound to record this. The romantic in me believes that history is written by the victors, so I am concerned by the dearth of books published by young, black South Africans.

Imagine growing up in a troubled land. As a carefree child, you do not know that anything is wrong. Then you start to become more socially and politically aware. You notice that there are places your family is forbidden to visit. You realise that the people on TV look nothing like you. You hear about people who leave and don't come back. They are only spoken of in whispers afterwards.

Then one morning you wake up and, without your knowing why, the world looks a bit brighter. People are dancing in the streets because a great man has been let out of prison. The freedom that people thought they would never see in their lifetime is a tantalising song on the wind, its gentle melody promising that nothing will ever be the same again.

The years roll on; that promise comes to fruition.

Sort of.

Citizens are free to roam all over their beloved country. There are new schools, new jobs and new friends. Previously unheard-of opportunities become available for all. We all fall in love with the idea of the rainbow nation.

But, a few more years down the road, many have become disillusioned. We have become two nations, and face challenges on a societal and economic level that we may not have anticipated in 1994.

I wanted to record our thoughts as the first generation to experience what it is like to live in a society that is situated, sometimes precariously, between a difficult past and a freer, though challenging, present. I think future generations would like to know how we coped with freedom and the legacies of the past – racism and poverty.

I waited for many years for someone to write about these things. When no one did, I knew I had to heed Toni Morrison's advice: 'If there's a book that you want to read, but it hasn't been written yet, then you must write it.'

Or, in this case, compile and contribute to it.

Twenty years later seems a good time to reflect on how events have affected us personally and collectively. It is in that spirit that I decided to compile this collection of essays. I've included essays dealing with a variety of themes, from the serious to the light-hearted. Essentially, it is a snapshot of what smart young South Africans think about living in this moment.

The book starts with a chapter in which contributors such as Shaka Sisulu describe aspects of life in South Africa today. This chapter also talks about phenomena that are unique to the democratic era, such as so-called black tax. Nama Xam writes a thought-provoking piece about our right to self-identify as African, and shares his feelings about discovering his Khoe heritage after having been classified as Coloured for so long.

The second chapter looks critically at race relations and Nelson Mandela's legacy. One can't write a book about South Africa without touching on racism and the legacy of apartheid, the (unwanted) gift that keeps on giving.

The third chapter moves on to a completely different topic: internet dating, lobola and kinky sex in a free country.

It is well known that education is the only way to break the poverty trap but, sadly, the democratic government has consistently failed to improve the lot of learners. In the fourth chapter, Simphiwe Dana suggests that mother-tongue teaching is one solution to the crisis in our education system, and Siphokuhle Mathe, a young student at the University of Cape Town (UCT), questions the deliberately slow pace of transformation and its implications for him.

For the fifth chapter, I called in the heavyweights – comedians David Kau, Loyiso Gola and Siv Ngesi, who offer comic relief in short vignettes.

We may have escaped apartheid's rigid classifications, but identity remains something we grapple with daily. How we view ourselves and the ways in which others try to pigeonhole us make for fascinating reading in the final chapter.

At this point, I also need to thank each talented human being who agreed to lend his or her voice to this project. It has taken about two years; there were days on which trying to get people to hand in essays made me feel like that Greek guy who kept rolling the rock up the same mountain. Thankfully, this book's story has a happy ending.

I hope it captures something of where we are as a nation now, and which issues and concerns are foremost in young black (meant in its most comprehensive way) South Africans' minds. If we are really lucky, this book will help to shape the debates currently taking place in workplaces and bars, and over dinner tables *ekasi* and in suburbs across the country.

YOLISA QUNTA

1

Different shades
of black

A story of privilege

SHAKA SISULU

Each generation must, out of relative obscurity,
discover its mission, fulfil it, or betray it.
Frantz Fanon

Many years ago, on a family vacation, I raised the ire of
the parental community. There were about 30 of us, span-
ning three generations, including more kids than any of
the adults were prepared to handle at once. After all, they
were on holiday.

Tempers frayed.

One day, as my cousins and I were running rambunc-
tiously through the chalets, slamming doors and knocking
over breakables, my aunty's shrill voice pierced the air.
Getting into trouble wasn't unfamiliar territory for me,
but her curse was particularly chilling: '*Hambani niyo
luka* (Get thee to initiation school)!'

The nearby elders all nodded in agreement. 'It is time,'
they mumbled among themselves, seeming to believe that
our conscription into initiation school would miraculously
turn us into responsible young men.

I wondered which special magic wand would be waved

there. But mostly, I worried about my own special magic wand, since the initiation process for young Xhosa men entails circumcision. Typically, this becomes the focal point of the entire process, but I soon discovered there was much more to it – just like a Bar Mitzvah is about more than wearing fancy clothes. Both play a key role in passing on aspects of group culture and a certain under-standing of the world.

Time passed and, before I knew it, the time of my induction into manhood was upon me. I went off with two cousins and returned some weeks later, filled with all kinds of ideas for how to face life's many challenges.

But what really astounded me was the reaction of the community. Suddenly, we were seen as adults. Just a few months earlier, we could technically not even sit at the same table as the grown-ups. I say technically, because our folks were somewhat liberal and didn't enforce this rule. Now, as grown men, we could – and were expected to – contribute to adult discussions on, well, just about anything.

Returning from initiation school is usually a time of celebration. Before the festivities end, every elderly man within earshot gets to add his tuppence of manly advice, ranging from the obvious to the more philosophical. What stood out was a great emphasis on the important role we were each expected to play in the community.

With our new-found respect came responsibility. We

were now not only responsible for ourselves and our families, but for the broader community as well.

Young men hear these sorts of things often, but rarely comprehend them. Nonetheless, the old men kept reminding us that the social and economic benefits that life would bestow upon us from time to time would be a result of the aid and support of others in our community, including our parents and grandparents and those unnamed elves who had aided and supported them. As such, we had a cultural duty to invest in a similar manner in the community and to help others where we could; we weren't islands.

And, like bird-watchers who had found a new twitching ground, the community flocked around us and did what grown-ups do – asked each other for help. In an economically depressed community in which one in four people was unemployed, this was inevitable. The responsibility, it seemed to me, engulfed us like a tidal wave.

More time passed and, with it – sadly – so did my beloved older brother Mlungisi. He'd recently married and was working as an accomplished diplomat in Sudan when he'd contracted cerebral malaria. Mlungisi was well loved and respected by all he came across. The elders were certainly impressed with how he dispensed his family responsibilities, because since my initiation, not once had I been required to do anything more than show up at family events and not make a nuisance of myself.

That all changed with Mlungisi's passing. The elders pulled me aside soon after his funeral and rattled off a list of responsibilities that I was now to assume, from the mundane make-sure-that-your-siblings-are-passing-at-school to the more treacherous intercede-in-family-quarrels. I was taken aback by the expectations that families had of their older children, and marvelled at how well my brother had quietly discharged his duties.

I imagined that he, too, had been given his assignments surreptitiously. I could see him emerging from clandestine meetings with the elders with a smile on his face that belied the seriousness of the discussions that had taken place inside. To us onlookers, such a sight would have been proof that the elders had all the fun and that sitting across from them at a table would be a special experience indeed.

Fans of mafia movies will recount the scene in *Goodfellas* when Tommy enters an empty room with glee, expecting to meet a counsel of godfathers ready to anoint him – only to get shot in the back of the head. We all want to get into the room to sit with the elders; we just don't know what it truly entails.

In any event, after my brother's death I began to have more and more meetings with my father and my uncles – sometimes individually, sometimes collectively. They piled on the assignments, which were small to start with but soon reached damn-near-impossible terrain.

This period of reassignments, even as we were still mourning the passing of a loved one, represented an innate process of succession planning, an institutionalised mechanism for manipulating natural selection in a family or clan's favour.

Importantly, I began to understand that with the prestige and privilege of sitting at the adult table came even more responsibility. It was like the sweet taste of a children's cough mixture, which only masks its real taste until it's down your throat. At least you know you'll feel better for it and, in time, you'll be able to take the medicine sans any flavouring.

That's the story of responsibility.

Privilege, anyone?

Many years ago, after I had completed my senior secondary schooling in Pretoria, I elected to leave for the Mother City. I had decided to enrol at the University of Cape Town (UCT) – the quality of their teaching and the worth of their degrees were legendary – but, more than anything, I wanted to live away from home in beautiful Cape Town.

I had been provisionally accepted based on my academic record. Soon afterwards, documentation stating this arrived in a big envelope with lots of prospectuses, tons of application forms and a number of schedules. I recall one schedule advising that I (and a guardian) travel to Cape Town to see the residences to book my place in one.

Somewhere in the same document the names of the school residence buildings were listed, with a description of the kind of lodging and catering arrangements available at each one.

Of course, not having any idea of what was what, my parents did what most parents who live miles away would do: they ticked the 'Select a res for me' box. 'Surely they wouldn't put our son into a hovel?' they must have reasoned, and I'm convinced they also said to each other, 'We're *definitely* not flying to Cape Town to select a residence! Who has money for *that*?'

When my mother and I had visited the university on a previous occasion for aptitude tests, we were shown around the campus and saw the wonderfully quaint on-campus lodgings. I'm sure that was the image in my mother's mind when she ticked that box. I couldn't care less – I was going to Cape Town!

The residence in which I found myself, along with all the other poor blokes whose parents had ticked that same box, was a good five kilometres from the main campus. A single hourly shuttle ran to the campus, but its hours didn't extend into the evening. I soon found out that other residences much closer to the campus had a number of shuttles every hour, and that they went on well into the evening. My res also lacked some computer and library-room facilities. I can't say much for the food either –but who in res can?

But worst of all was the immediately palpable segregation – our residence was all black. As in, every resident was black. Of course, the institution didn't see anything racist in this – they were simply following a rote that ensured children from certain schools were given priority access to certain residences. I would learn that over the years, a relationship had developed between some schools and the university, both of which were attended and funded by products of the same old boys' (and girls') networks.

The other aspect of this was less malevolent than insidious. Many of the students in the better living quarters closer to the main campus had applied very early on, much earlier than the application forms for residences went out. They had somehow been privy to the system – or, rather, they were inside a network of people who were. Many of their parents, uncles or older siblings had been to UCT themselves, and knew the ropes.

That alumni would be overwhelmingly white in the 1990s was a fact that seemed to escape the administrative staff at the time. Consequently, the residence with the fewest amenities had only black occupants and was even dubbed 'the township' by many of its residents.

These students, and the administrators who kept this system intact, were seemingly blind to the reality of intergenerational privilege. You see, this is the very essence of privilege: it isn't stark to the person it favours, but is noticeable to the chaps who aren't in the same position.

This all became clear to me when I went to hang out with my friends in other residences. Many of them never visited us in our res because it was ostensibly too far away – and since we had to pass their res on our way to campus anyway . . . So, many of the more privileged residents never quite understood the extent of their privilege. They never saw the other side and, for some reason, we who lived furthest away didn't really speak about it.

At the time, such things were only mentioned when one was angry and there was a spontaneous protest at the res or when a couple of the more politicised students took the matter up in their student politics. They expected me to join them because I had a political surname and was 'suffering' the same ignobility. However, I was too busy doing what most underprivileged classes do: making do.

And being cool. Too cool to protest.

Years later, when the urge to get involved in things that extended beyond my own circumstances emerged, I was still very cool. So cool, in fact, that I'd get many an invitation to the popular Joburg kids' parties. We were mostly in our twenties and had begun to come into our own, especially financially. We had few responsibilities and, therefore, some disposable income. And, of course, time. Lots of time.

It was at one such a party that a beautiful girl with an illustrious background – she was of cultural and political royalty – invited me to a special kind of event. A 'build', she called it. I obliged, knowing full well which other popular kids and especially beautiful young ladies would be there. I made sure to go, even though I was severely hung over at the time.

It was one of my life's defining moments. Years later, I would realise that on that day, when I could think of nothing more than adventure, having fun and pursuing ladies, the seed for Cheesekids for Humanity was planted in me. I was about to realise that not only was I privileged, but also that I had forgotten exactly how fortunate I was. Some time after that I founded Cheesekids, a non-governmental organisation (NGO) that aims to mobilise and bring young people together in community service.[1]

Over time, I came to understand that I could leverage my privilege and empower other members of my community to rise up the social ladder, simply by giving what I had a lot of then – time.

Even though we are taught that we aren't islands, it dawned on me that those of us who have social privilege don't, largely, understand the extent of it. South Africa, which now has the highest Gini coefficient in the world, requires that those with privilege assume a position in society as elders who have a significant responsibility to intervene in the country's structural imbalances.

---

1 Cheesekids encourages volunteerism and, unbeknown to the participants, develops them into young leaders by simply making community service fun, easy and accessible.

Many of us will need rites of passage or protocols demanding that we assume our responsibility – that we face our privilege, and then figure out how to use it to change the future of those whose only sin is to have been born in poverty.

If we as the privileged classes – those who have gone to better schools, whose parents have worked hard to give them better opportunities, those who have made a name or money for themselves or who are politically connected – do not assume our gargantuan responsibilities in this country and on this continent, then we would have failed in Fanon's generational mission.

If we do not accept this role, we may be successful on the surface, but will, in fact, be failures.

Ain't nobody got time for that.

The eternal intern

SEITISO NTLOTHEBE

One of the most painful experiences in my life journey so far has been hearing the voice of my mother, Mme Sebusang Bodike, ululating over the phone shortly before announcing to my two younger siblings, Tsholofelo and Neo, that I had found a job.

'*O ngwanake! O bone tiro. Re tla kgona go bona botshelo* (My child has found a job. Finally, we too shall begin to live life joyously).'

Mother sounded so very relieved. Now she, too, would begin to command respect in her community as the order of things in our society stipulates. Securing a job brought some kind of dignity; now that I, Botlhale, *leitibolo la ga Mme Mma Bodike* (Mma Bodike's first-born) had found work, this is what my mother believed. Embarrassed, and afraid to ruin what sounded like a convivial moment at home, I purposely omitted to mention that it was yet another internship.

My fourth one.

Ever since I'd left university, I'd been hopping from one internship programme to another like a kangaroo. I'd had to watch as my mates had started to lead cushy lives filled with all manner of luxuries. They'd bought cars made by the very best manufacturers in Europe, and had rented or bought houses in leafy suburbs such as Sandton, Midrand and Fourways.

Meanwhile, at the end of every twelve-month cycle, I would hear the same clichéd excuses. 'I am very sorry, Botlale (they meant Botlhale; not that they cared), but we cannot accommodate you on a permanent basis.'

After the second or third time, I'd considered taking my own life. What is the purpose of this kind of existence? I'd asked myself. But then I'd thought of my mother, for whom I have so much respect, and my siblings, the cute twins who, their young age notwithstanding, seemed to have understood the pain I'd been going through and had drawn inspiration from my strength. I'd known I was a role model, not only to Neo and Tsholofelo, but also to my mother. In their eyes, I was a beacon of hope.

What I understood perfectly well is that I represented their ticket out of poverty, misery and humiliation. I knew that the salary I would earn if I ever got that job I yearned for would not be mine alone. However small my income, I would have to send half of it home. This is not only the expectation of my family, but of most black families around the country. History had seen to it that things would be that way.

Fortunately, in my moments of darkness, sanity has always prevailed. I realised that I had to live, even if it meant suffering, so that my loved ones could have a glimpse of a better life. Besides, I could not reconcile myself with being known as a coward in death.

Despite this being my fourth internship, I was also partially relieved. The last time I'd had any kind of employment was eighteen months before. While the pocket money, to which employers refer as a salary, would be less than I'd been paid for my previous internment over a year ago, it would be better than nothing, I convinced myself. This is something at which you become quite adept: convincing yourself that everything will be all right. It is a language in which I – Botlhale, daughter of Mme Mma Bodike – have become fluent.

It beats sitting at home with no income.

At some point, I'd applied for teaching positions, thinking that my degree in Geology would enable me to teach Mathematics and Science. The answer: I was overqualified, or there was no job for me. Word on the street was that the local teaching staff had been threatened by what they perceived as my fancy city education.

'*Bare o tla ba tseela tiro* (They mentioned that you would steal their jobs),' a little bird whispered to me. It was ridiculous – my goal was to put bread on the table to feed my family and, most importantly, to plough back into my community.

For months, I was the butt of jokes in my home village of Itireleng, a rural town about 100 kilometres west of Vryburg in North West. Translated directly into the Queen's English, Itireleng means 'do it for yourself', but perhaps 'help yourself' makes more sense. The name amuses me still, because in Itireleng almost no one cares about improving their livelihoods, let alone those of their fellow community members.

My tertiary education at the University of the Witwatersrand started haunting me. In the minds of my tormentors, it became a weapon of choice – a preamble to their mockery of my privilege.

'*Ya cleva! Akere one ore wena o rutegile o ka se nne le rona mo magaeng. Ke fa jaanong o tlabame mo gae o tshwana le rona* (Hey, genius! You thought yourself too educated to live in a village. Now here you are, languishing with us in this rot),' they would say as they gave each other high-fives and laughed raucously.

The whole village knew that Mme Mma Bodike's smart and well-mannered daughter had gone to university, studied and graduated with a Bachelor of Science (Honours) in Geology; but now she was back home.

'Look at her now. Jobless and useless', they murmured.

Rumours began to circulate that I hadn't actually graduated.

'*Bare le go aloga, ga aloga* (Apparently she did not even finish university)', one said.

'*Nnyaa, re bone ditshwantsho tsa gagwe a apere kobo ya thuto* (No, but we saw her graduation ceremony pictures),' the second one argued.

But the third one quickly interjected: '*Hee tsala, a o itse* technology *sentle?! Ke utlwile ka selo gatwe* Photoshop (My friend, do not underestimate the power of technology. Have you never heard of Photoshop)?'

Some rumours were even more malicious. I even heard that I'd had to quit school because I'd fallen pregnant and had abandoned the baby.

'Exquisite and mesmerising. It is as if God escapes here whenever he needs a break from the unending politics and boardrooms of heaven and earth.'

I once overheard a tourist, American if her accent was anything to go by, rave in this way about our country. She was right. South Africa is a most beautiful country. But experiencing its splendour depends almost entirely on your position on the socio-economic ladder, which – in turn – is determined by the atrocious sins of the past. To this day, those sins continue to haunt me.

I always hear from foreigners how wonderful our country is: of Cape Town's irrepressible beauty with the glorious Table Mountain overlooking the Atlantic Ocean. But if Table Mountain could speak, it would tell of the arrival of that Dutch barbarian Jan van Riebeeck and his band of thugs. Some may not want to hear it, but we are doing future generations no favours by hiding the truth.

The words of that tourist playing in my head, I was filled with rage. I recalled two passages from the famous speech by that great son of the soil Thabo Mbeki, aptly entitled 'I am an African'. Mbeki said: 'I owe my being to the Khoi and the San whose desolate souls haunt the great expanses of the beautiful Cape – they who fell victim to the most merciless genocide our native land has ever seen, they who were the first to lose their lives in the struggle to defend our freedom and dependence and they who, as a people, perished in the result.'

But it was the passage that followed that made me boil with anger. In it, Mbeki berates the hypocrites who wished for black people to be slapped by amnesia's heavy hand and forget about the despicable deeds of the past while selfishly holding on to the country's wealth. He said: 'Today, as a country, we keep an audible silence about these ancestors of the generations that live, fearful to admit the horror of a former deed, seeking to obliterate from our memories a cruel occurrence which, in its remembering, should teach us not and never to be inhuman again.'

Mbeki is right, I thought. The only way to sort out our problems in South Africa is by acknowledging the elephant in the room. By ignoring it, those whose progenitors travelled to our shores for the sole purpose of pillaging do not have to feel uncomfortable about their wealth. Why do we keep up the pretence that all is well in South Africa?

I recalled a profound statement by Sizwe, one of my university friends who, for a Computer Science major, had a surprisingly penetrating interest in history, literature, politics and philosophy. He'd once remarked that, 'We do not want to upset our masters in the West, lest they decide to rain bombs down on us like they so often do in the Middle East. So, we smile politely at those who hold their ill-gotten loot tightly.'

When the call came from Johannesburg that day inviting me to an interview, I was so excited that my ears let me down. I did not hear that it was not a permanent position but yet another gruesome twelve-month internship programme, one of the government's Band-Aid solutions to the ever-worsening problem of youth unemployment. I had had enough of rural Itireleng and its destructive gossip.

Mme Mma Sebusang Bodike – a truly kind soul – gave me almost all of her remaining monthly allowance so I could catch a taxi to Vryburg, where I would get onto another taxi that would take me to the bright lights of Johannesburg – a place known to my mother only in her limitless imagination.

'Your mother is a brilliant woman. You are just like her. Pity the brutality and hatred of the previous regime limited her to the village of Itireleng. Promise me that you will never let anything stand in your way, my child. Leave this village and see the world,' my father, Rre Tuelo Petrus Bodike, once told me.

Unfortunately, when I'd begun my first year at Wits eight years ago, my father had joined the non-living. The little that sustains our family comes from the money he left behind. A miner in Rustenburg, he had secured from his employers the bursary that had enabled me to study at Wits. They had promised to employ me after I'd completed my studies. I have yet to hear from them.

Now Mma Bodike was sharing some of her late husband's money with me so I could travel to my interview. Oh, Mme Mma Bodike. She is not of this world, with a heart so pure it is capable only of love and compassion. She had made me seven-colours cake to eat on my journey to the big city on that particularly warm Sunday.

When the driver started the taxi to signal that it was about to depart, my mother, the widow of Oom Petrus – as my father had affectionately been known – flashed a heartfelt smile, a tear of hope and joy running down what was once a beautiful face.

'*Tsamaya le Modimo ngwanaka* (May the Lord be with you, my child),' she said as she waved goodbye.

The silver-grey Toyota Quantum rattled into motion. It took to the white gravel road that would later join a tarred road, or *sekontere*, as it known in Itireleng. As I journeyed through the platinum-rich province of North West, I wished not to return home.

I left on a Sunday so I could have enough time to prepare for the interview, which was scheduled for that Tuesday afternoon. Student friends offered accommodation.

Now, a few metres outside the premises of the company I had just gone to for the interview, I am on the phone, listening patiently – albeit with some embarrassment – to Mme Mma Bodike rejoicing in my 'achievement'. A woman of limited education, she had nonetheless come to learn what 'internship programme' means – a term that had turned her first-born into a modern slave. In 1994, a cake of hope had been baked with the promise that her daughter would get a slice. But when it was ready, all she'd received was crumbs.

Hearing the joy and relief in her voice, I cannot bear the thought of cutting her happiness short.

Not just an ID

NAMA XAM

Unlike a drop of water which loses its identity when it
joins the ocean, man does not lose his being in the society
in which he lives. Man's life is independent.
He is born not for the development of the society alone,
but for the development of his self.
BR Ambedkar

The words in this quote will ring true to anyone who is
on a journey of self-discovery, as I am. My journey is that
of a human being classified as 'Coloured' in post-apartheid South Africa.

As a child born on the Cape Flats in the seventies, I
experienced the tail end of the liberation struggle – the
rubber bullets and teargas, the demonstrations and being chased by the police and defence force. I grew up in a
household of four. My father was a working man who had
left school at a young age to work so his family could eat.
My mother was a teacher who had built herself up from
humble beginnings to educate the next generation. I have
an older brother whose calm and quiet demeanour sometimes causes people to underestimate him.

My political foundation was based on the principle that

life was about the people and for the people. I'd been taught that positive change was paramount for growth in the country, and that this could be attained through love and self-sacrifice. Still, as a young boy my search for cultural initiation to manhood led me down the path that so many young men and women in township communities follow: gangsterism. Fortunately, I wasn't drawn in permanently; in about 1990, I was baptised into a movement that focused my journey of self-discovery. I became a child of hip hop.

This explosive culture originated in the ghettos of New York. It gave me, a child of the Cape Flats, an outlet to express the frustration of not having had the space to explore who I was. Spinning on my head, spraying a wall or speaking in rhyme allowed me to discover life and grow my mind.

As so many have said before, hip hop is about having fun and forgetting, if only for a moment, the struggles we face. Hip hop also opened my eyes to our limitless potential through its forms of expression – breakdancing (whose roots can be traced back to Africa), graffiti (bringing to mind Khoe Khoen and San rock and cave paintings), beatboxing (the original instrument), turntablism (the break), MCing (the MC as speaker, poet, teacher and leader), and others that have been added in recent times.

The element of hip hop that, I feel, gives rise to all of these forms of expression is KOS – knowledge of self. You cannot share anything with others if you have no clue about who you are. So, as b-boys, graf writers, DJs, beatboxers and MCs, we acquired information about our ancestry as African people. We also found material from covert sources about the white supremacist system. Many deemed distributing this information an act of rebellion; we were ostracised, even by our own communities, but this information empowered me with a sense of worth and pride and fuelled my spirit.

I was classified as different, but I liked it.

A hip hop community consists of many different personalities and energies. I was fortunate to connect with Bradlox Vans, the MC, poet, teacher and cultural activist. He had also started a journey of rediscovering his culture.

Before 1994, as a so-called Cape Coloured I was bombarded with propaganda about my bastardised heritage and identity, supposedly born from ghetto or township culture. This 'culture' was subtly promoted as the only heritage of 'Coloured' people. I believe this propaganda intended to disown the descendants of the aboriginal peoples, the Khoe Khoen and Bushmen, of this area to prevent them from laying claim to land.

During this time, I also discovered that my father's lineage went back to the Nama Khoe, and that it is customary in African culture for a son to follow his father's line. *Tita ge Nama Khoe* – I am a Nama person.

So it came to be that with Bradlox and some other like-minded people, I started a non-profit organisation called the Khoe Khoen and San Active Awareness Group (KSAAG). The vision and mission of this group is to inform, educate and mobilise people with Khoe Khoen heritage. We had no intentions of forming a new tribe or becoming chiefs of sheep; we initiated the distribution of reading and listening material pertaining to the Nama Gowab (Nama language), one of the most commonly spoken Khoe Khoen dialects.

A delegation from our organisation attended a gathering of the Nama Khoe in Gibeon, Namibia. There, they met the paramount chief Hendrik Witbooi VIII, who shared insight into the movement of the Nama Khoe. He told us that they moved from their old home – the Cape (//Hui !Gaeb, Where the Clouds Gather) – to their new home in Namibia. Through my interaction with the Nama Khoe and 'Coloured' people, I've realised the extent of colonial South Africa's ethnocide campaign and the continual onslaught against the Khoe Khoen and Bushman people.

The words 'Khoe Khoen' mean 'Person of People'. I have reservations about the word 'Khoisan' as an umbrella term for the indigenous Khoe Khoen and Bushman people of South Africa, as Khoisan is not a word in the Khoe Khoen or Bushman languages. It is a term first used by someone who could not pronounce the words correctly. So, using 'Khoisan' to describe us implies that we as a people are starting from a place of distortion and confusion again, as with the term 'Coloured'.

For more than a decade, my journey has intensified with the rediscovery of my culture and identity. However, my journey has also opened my eyes to the problems with group cultures. What I have realised is that, in today's society, the concept of identity is manipulated to favour group identity. I understand the importance of unity as a people, but that unity should reflect a consciousness that is not internally destructive to the masses. It should also stem from creation and upliftment.

This is the space in which I find myself. I have standards, principles, foundations, goals and a belief system to ensure a true vision of the sustainability of self, even though I may be isolated at times. I believe in the power of self-love. After all, how can you love another, if you cannot love yourself?

I figure that I am an ME (meaningful entity).

Not just an ID (identity deemed).

Toa Tama !Khams Ge (the struggle continues).

The gift of hope

THANDO NTOI

His jaw dropped and his eyes widened. My father could not believe what he was hearing. I had just told him I was planning to quit my job.

He asked me again if something had happened. A disagreement with my boss, perhaps? The team? The company culture?

No, I said. I am just not happy.

My father's disbelief isn't difficult to understand. He was born in 1951 and raised in the township of Orlando, Soweto, by a single mother who worked as a domestic worker. In the South Africa into which he and his seven siblings had been born, individual destiny and the pursuit of happiness for black people were unheard of.

Black women, in particular, endured the most challenging circumstances. The combination of the apartheid state and patriarchal culture kept them shackled, unable to construct the lives to which they aspired. If you were fortunate enough to secure employment, you held onto it for dear life; here I was, a gainfully employed young black woman who was about to quit her job.

I could try to claim to be a pioneer, but I was walking a path that had already been trodden by a number of legendary South African women. Women like the 20 000 who had marched to the Union Buildings on 9 August 1956, some with their children strapped to their backs. Women who'd not only had the courage to protest against a regime that had thwarted opposition in the past, but who'd also had the grace to do so in a peaceful, orderly manner.

These women were the urban embodiment of the rural women who held households and families together while their men were forced to toil in distant and unwelcoming cities – women at the forefront of the struggle to end apartheid, who risked more than just their lives. Many endured rape and torture.

In 1994, when apartheid ended and a democratic South Africa was taking shape, I was a chubby thirteen-year-old undergoing some awkward changes of my own. I was just starting high school; the pressure to decide what I wanted to do with my life was starting to mount. My parents were so excited for me. They kept telling me that it was the 'new South Africa' now; I could do anything my heart desired. Provided, of course, it would make me money.

By December 1996, I still had not decided what I wanted to study when I finished high school. Standard 8 (Grade 10) was fast approaching. I had to select my subjects. In the same month, President Nelson Mandela promulgated the Constitution of South Africa, still considered to be one of the most progressive in the world. The Constitution's Bill of Rights outlined the freedoms I could enjoy and the rights I could demand.

However, the reach of the Constitution did not appear to extend to our house. My parents made it clear that my freedom to choose school subjects did not include dropping Maths and Science.

By 2004, as South Africa celebrated a decade of freedom, I had almost completed my degree in commerce. It started out as a degree in information systems, but had morphed into a degree specialising in business finance and accounting as the years had progressed. I was convinced that I had discovered exactly what I wanted to do. My parents had been right: I wanted to make money!

My career started soon thereafter in a sprawling bank in the heart of Johannesburg's central business district. By the second year of my tenure as a programme manager, I realised that a change was necessary. I found the work monotonous and began to feel that I was no longer learning anything. Fortuitously, an ambitious director at the bank who was leaving to start a corporate finance boutique had noticed my talents. I wasted no time in signing on the dotted line. My second career as a corporate finance analyst began.

Then, the financial crisis of 2008 happened. It was a difficult time for boutique financial services companies still finding their feet; I had to forge a new path for myself to put bread on the table. Not willing to be exposed in such a way again, I opted for stability and joined the corporate finance division of one of the so-called Big Four audit firms.

Four years and an honours degree later, I realised – once again – that I needed a change. My ultimate aspiration now was to own and run my own business. In corporate finance we had worked on a project basis, going into different businesses and analysing them for sale and valuation purposes. I felt I needed experience in the actual running of a business, which I did not believe I would get in corporate finance.

I joined a large insurance company as part of a pro-gramme to attract young, black, female professionals. Our group underwent vigorous training and I was unleashed into the business as strategy and innovation manager. And so I entered a third career.

I had a great boss. He was encouraging, and a good mentor – someone who took on a paternal role and guided me through the business to help me find my niche. My colleagues were also warm and welcoming. One even became a very close friend. I really liked the company. But, one year later, having earned the chartered financial analyst designation, I realised that this was also not for me.

44

This time around, I knew what – or rather, who – the problem was. When I voiced my inclination to leave, the company offered me other opportunities within the business, but I had to tell them: it's not you, it's me.

I needed time to figure out what I really wanted to do. Being a prudent financial professional, I had sufficient savings to take some time off. It was against this backdrop that I had the conversation with my father. After receiving his reluctant blessing, I stepped into the great unknown.

I was scared, but not petrified. I was no longer living in the South Africa that my father remembered. It was 2013; my country was on the cusp of celebrating twenty years of democracy. Much had changed. I found myself in a South Africa that was full of opportunities for a young professional like me. I rationalised that even if I did not fare well as an entrepreneur, I could always go back to a corporate job. After all, I had sought-after qualifications and years of experience. I considered myself highly employable. In addition, I was a black woman.

Today, policies are in place to address the imbalances of the past. From being at the very bottom of the metaphorical totem poll, black women are theoretically now on top. With the correct qualifications and the right attitude, very little can hold us back.

The results are starting to show. A 2014 report by international audit firm Grant Thornton revealed that women fill 28 per cent of senior management positions in South

African businesses. This is a far cry from the government's target of 50 per cent, but it is line with other developing countries – specifically the BRICS countries – and is higher than global average of 24 per cent.

In the public sector, South Africa is ranked eighth out of 188 countries in terms of female representation in Parliament. Women constitute 42 per cent of South Africa's Parliament. More than half of all university students are women, and women represent more than half of all graduates despite South Africa's alarming dropout rate.

We have come a long way from the kitchen. Nevertheless, there are still numerous challenges to surmount. Even though more women than men graduate from university, South African women experience higher unemployment than men. Most of the people living below the poverty line in South Africa are women. Those women who do secure employment earn, on average, 33 per cent less than their male colleagues who perform the same jobs.

Safety is still a significant challenge for the majority of South African women. Interpol has called South Africa the rape capital of the world. The statistics are horrifying, and are likely to be an underestimation as most rapes go unreported. Intimate femicide, the killing of women by their partners, is the leading cause of female homicide in South Africa; three women are killed by their partners every single day.

However, these challenges have not gone unnoticed. In

an attempt to address the scourge of violence against women, the Department of Justice is reintroducing courts dedicated to handling sexual offences. By 2014, 22 such courts had been established and the Minister of Justice and Correctional Services had announced that 106 more courts would be established over the next ten years. Whether these measures will succeed is yet to be determined, but I am hopeful.

And that is exactly what I told my father, once he had regained his composure. I told him that even with full knowledge of all the realities we face in our country, I remain hopeful – because I have grown alongside an emerging South Africa and have watched it transform itself from a country that kept women entrapped and unhappy to one in which women like me have the opportunity to chase their dreams.

This wonderful nation has enabled me, slowly but steadily, to creep up Maslow's hierarchy to a place where self-actualisation is a real possibility.

I couldn't tell my father right then what I would be doing in the immediate future. I could be running a small business, starting yet another career, or even begging for my old job back, but I was excited.

Freedom means different things to different people. For me, it is the ability to live my life with hope.

2

What have we struggled for?

Spider's web

YOLISA QUNTA

There I was, sitting in the bright interior of a popular restaurant, drinking overpriced tea, when I heard a commotion behind me. I turned around to see that all the waiters had congregated around a table and were banging rhythmically on their trays. Then, they broke into song: 'Happy birthday' to the tune of 'Shosholoza'.

At that moment, all the other patrons turned to look. Some even whipped out their phones and started recording. Just like that, the reality of race relations in South Africa intruded on my innocuous morning drink in the leafy suburbs.

As I looked at those singers, my first instinct was to feel discomfort. Not the sort to make me run screaming into the street; no, it was more subtle than that. As I looked around the room, I realised that, aside from our two-seater, all of the patrons were white. And all of the singers were African. Weren't we decades away from the help singing plantation lullabies to entertain the white folk? Sure, I may have overreacted – but given that certain white people still think it's a compliment to tell African people that they speak 'good English', my reaction should not come as a surprise.

I grew up surrounded by adults who took the business of liberating South Africa very seriously. I was a struggle baby, so to speak: both of my parents were part of liberation movements and I knew that one day I, too, would be. My plan was to finish high school, go for military training and then go on to university to study something useful to the struggle.

Then 1994 happened when I was thirteen; it seemed I was going to grow up like a normal teenager. I was quite happy to pass through the normal teenage rituals – falling in love, and starting minor rebellions of my own.

But it seems I was cursed with the affliction of always wanting to do the right thing. Even though I could not articulate exactly what it was, something about the carefully packaged transition from apartheid to freedom through Codesa and the Truth and Reconciliation Commission's all too brief attempt at being a Band-Aid rankled me.

When I was about seventeen, I asked my mother what the mission of our generation was now that we were free. I felt strongly that, as a generation who was benefiting from living in freedom, we should remain aware of apartheid's legacy and our obligation to take further strides.

I vaguely remember my mother responding that although we were free, the struggle was not over.

Fast forward many years, and I have become aware that South Africa's greatest challenge is also the one that is least acknowledged: racism. Unfortunately, I can say from personal experience that the ghost of apartheid is alive and well. Here are a few examples of how I have seen it manifest itself:

1. The hard-of-hearing saleswoman

One day, strolling through the mall, I came across a Karen Millen store. My heart beat a joyful tune: I no longer had to travel to London to acquire exquisite clothes. A vision of perfection in navy caught my eye; I knew there and then that I had to have it.

I asked the shop assistant whether she had it in a size twelve. Instead of looking for a dress that would fit my wonderful curves, she replied by giving me the price of the item. I was confused, but assumed that years of listening to Lady Gaga full blast through her cellphone headset had affected her hearing.

Then I asked my question again: this time I was sure to repeat it slowly and clearly. At this point, she stopped mentioning prices, deigned to inform me that the dress was 'expensive', and enquired whether I was sure I could afford it.

All I could do was turn around and walk out.

I defer to the patron saint of scorned shoppers everywhere, one Miss Vivian: 'Big mistake. Huge.'

2. The statistician security guard

Your parents were right to insist that you focus at school. Education is a truly wonderful and empowering tool that will take you places. Sometimes, it even gives you powers that seem mystical to the untrained observer.

Take, for instance, the moment when you are stopped for a 'random' search, or you find yourself being followed around a store by a security guard, and you realise that you are the only person with a darker skin colour in the vicinity. In the interests of fairness, you try to engage said security guard in a discussion about the merits of the Monte Carlo methods or to have a chat about independent variables, since you had wrestled with Stats 101 at some stage at varsity.

At this point, you discover that your homie is actually an expert in entomology, because all you hear is crickets.

3. The advertising exec who moonlights as a choreographer

Firstly, I need to point out that I'm not a party pooper. I love to dance, and can think of quite a few scenarios that would make me *twalatsa* with the best of them. If I won the lotto, I would spontaneously break into a cha-cha. When Idris Elba finally asks me to marry him, you'd better believe that I will do a spectacular victory dance past every well-meaning girlfriend who has ever told me that my obsession with him was unrealistic. I really don't have a problem with dancing.

What truly irks me is the narrative that white advertisers are pushing: that black people will dance for just about any reason. Switch on your TV on any night of the week and you will see women old enough to be your grandmother dancing in paroxysms of joy over a Kit Kat or men you would call *bhuti* gyrating because of five rand's worth of airtime.

The reason for this is quite simple. There is a field in which white people in advertising grow all the fucks they give when it comes to respecting black people and their culture. Right now, that field is bare. As in completely empty. A veritable wasteland.

Think about that the next time you're shopping or when your kids ask why Makhulu is twerking about a certain brand of chips.

4. The classist doorman

Whenever the debate about whether Cape Town is a racist city comes up, so does the issue of how black patrons are treated at bars and restaurants. It seems you can't take more than three steps without meeting a person of colour – from an award-winning DJ to a lowly social drinker – who has been a victim of apartheid-style door policies.

I had first-hand experience of this at Asoka. Back in the day, I was a regular patron. I liked it for many reasons – firstly, because it was open all week and each day had a different vibe. Then there was the Porn Star Martini, a delicious concoction with fresh passion fruit and a shot of bubbly that tasted like more. Add to that a friendly bartender who knew my favourites, and was able to serve them after a few finger-waves from the back of the three-deep crowd, and you can see why I kept going back.

Then, one day during the 2010 Soccer World Cup, I was denied entry in exactly the same way as all those other black people I refused to believe. Of course, I e-mailed the owner, but got whitesplaining, mostly, and a laughable apology that had he known it had been me at the door, things would have been different. I wrote an article about my experience, which went viral. I have still not been back.

There will be people who try to negate my and other black Capetonians' experiences at restaurants and bars by claiming classism rather than racism. I beg to differ. Sadly, black people who don't love themselves keep going to these places and are still getting the same treatment today.

5. The online troll

Anyone who is familiar with Tolkien mythology will know trolls. These unpleasant creatures have very little intelligence, are rather inarticulate, are not particularly attractive and turn into stone at sunrise.

Online trolls have much the same characteristics, but, sadly, are impervious to the sun's rays. They trawl the dark alleys of the interwebs from the safe anonymity of their keyboards, spilling their vitriol among their ilk. These losers hide behind the mask of free speech. Online companies are mostly too cowardly to expose them even when they are clearly intent on causing harm.

But I say they should all be exposed. The last thing mild-mannered Bob wants his family and friends to know is that, under cover of darkness, he transforms online into a rabid fascist, homophobe, or sexual deviant.

The common denominator in all of these scenarios, barring the last one, is that they are so insidious that, to the casual observer, they may appear as if nothing is amiss – or as incidents in which I had simply experienced a combination of stupidity and poor customer service.

Trying to explain racist incidents to people who have never been exposed to racism themselves, or who choose to remain oblivious to it, feels like walking into a spider's web. There's the all-too-familiar flailing as you try to disentangle yourself from the invisible skeins. But even though it might look like nothing from the outside, the person inside the web is acutely aware that something is wrong.

News reports tell us that overtly racist incidents happen across the country every day. This suggests that something is bubbling under the surface of our collective psyche, something that could burst horribly if things continue as they are. A first step could be deep introspection on both sides. Being made to feel as if you are imagining things doesn't help.

As black South Africans, we need to admit that we are angry and have every reason to be. The next step is to take ownership if we want to be change agents and to challenge racism actively whenever we encounter it. This is not easy – some days, you really just want to take the skinny latte and hold the side order of racist bullshit.

Until we teach people how to treat us and are prepared to articulate exactly why specific behaviour is not okay, we will never feel comfortable in our own country.

In this, we have to keep in mind that being economically empowered plays a major role in how comfortable you are about speaking up. As a middle-class black person with an education, it is easy for me to tell off service providers and send strongly worded e-mails to corporate head offices to get my point across. However, if I were working for a pittance as a maid, I would probably not tell my employer how much her refusal to use my Xhosa name, because she finds it too hard to say, offends me.

Until black people in this country are economically empowered, equality will remain a pipe dream. It's very easy for us to pat ourselves on the collective back for being a free country, but without economic freedom people are barred from so many things.

Let us look at an example: getting a tertiary education. Suppose a black student gets university exemption, despite the quality of public schools in townships and rural areas, and miraculously finds himself or herself accepted into a higher-education institution. He or she will have to pay thousands upfront in registration fees. Residence fees need paying. And then there's the matter of acquiring textbooks, which start at R300 each. A middle-class student's parents would pay the fees or stand surety for a student loan. So, whereas in theory working-class black students are free to attend a university of their choice, in reality the option is simply priced out of their reach.

This is why white South Africans who profess their non-racism on a daily basis should check their privilege and do some serious introspection. Firstly, if they truly love this country they need to stop the knee-jerk, not-all-whites-are-like-that reaction whenever one of their own is found to be acting unacceptably. Secondly, Nelson Mandela's greatest legacy seems to have been that of bestowing the majority of white South Africans with the gift of collective amnesia. This gift has allowed them to forget exactly how they earned their white privilege. They are very quick to claim that times have changed and that we should move on; they could start by admitting that apartheid's unfair advantage will probably be passed on to the next four generations of white children.

At this point, I should probably start offering solutions. If I had any, I would probably be in Parliament right now, taking credit for them. So, there will be no glib quick fixes from me.

However, I do have a parting thought. As black South Africans, it is up to all of us to push for economic empowerment as soon as possible: less reconciliation, more reparation. Give back the stolen land; redistribute mineral rights to those to whom they rightfully belong. According to Census 2011, Africans make up 79.2 per cent of the population.[2] In 2012, a study commissioned by the JSE found that direct ownership by this population group was 8.9 per cent.[3] It's somewhat harder to get land ownership figures but according to a PLAAS report, white commercial farmers own about 67 per cent of agricultural land.[4] These figures paint a very bleak picture of how far behind economically the majority of the population is.

Only then can we talk to our white compatriots from a place of equal power and find real solutions, instead of directing black anger at deaf white privilege.

---

2 http://www.southafrica.info/about/people/population.htm#.VwNLI_197IX

3 http://www.plaas.org.za/sites/default/files/publications-pdf/No1%20Fact%20check%20web.pdf

4 http://venturesafrica.com/jse-still-white-owned-say-black-experts/

The first revolution was about overthrowing apartheid and all forms of oppression. After 22 years, it is clear that this longed-for freedom has not trickled down. Most people who look like us still live in abject poverty and are held back by structural oppression.

As black people who have benefited from the post-1994 dispensation, we have an even greater incentive to bring about change: the next revolution will take place when our kinsfolk get tired of hearing 'not yet *uhuru*' and forcibly take their due. There is no certainty that, in their righteous anger, they will distinguish between their former oppressors and those of us who have benefited since 1994 but have done nothing to help them. Unlike our Caucasian counterparts, however, we won't have the luxury of running off to Australia.

This is why we need to work overtime to fix this broken system – or be swept away in the coming tide.

Times are changing

LWANDILE FIKENI

The first time I read Steve Biko's *I write what I like*, I was lying naked next to a woman in her university residence room. It was the morning after, I'd reached for one of a handful of books on her bedside table.

Reading the first few essays in Biko's book left me terribly nervous. As a black student at Wits in the early 2000s, his condition was familiar to me. Lost in the corridors of whiteness, questions of race and identity preoccupied my and my fellow black students' minds. I was sixteen, and on my way to dropping out of a BCom (Accounting) degree.

Growing up in the former Transkei, we didn't preoccupy ourselves with whites. We were a homeland – a Bantustan – and few whites in our town were neighbourly. In many ways, they had assimilated into our culture. Generally, whites in the Transkei knew how to behave, and still do. I suspect it's due to the idyll of the lush Wild Coast, the famous rolling hills of the Mbhashe, and the respect that Xhosa culture demands of those who coexist with Xhosa people. We called elderly black women and men 'Mama' and 'Tata' respectively. It was 'Sir' and 'Ma'am' for our white and Coloured neighbours. Whites learnt our language (to a commendable degree), lived in our neighbourhoods and went with us to school.

Once I got to university, however, I realised two things. Firstly, whites were evidently more privileged than blacks. Secondly, the peaceful race relations I was used to were not a reality at Wits. Violent incidents took place. A black student would be attacked by a group of white students, with no punishment meted out to the perpetrators. The white students would continue to attend class, with a smugness that betrayed their knowing something we didn't.

And I guess, to some extent, they did. These were the dynamics of South Africa: whites were accustomed to being superior to blacks. I must confess, this was something I wasn't used to. My only exposure to it had been on trips to East London, when my mother and I would go to visit my gran who owned a shebeen in Mdantsane.

Although East London (near the former Ciskei) was in our back yard, we'd have to cross the border into South Africa to go there. At the Nciba border, now called the Kei Bridge, we'd suffered terror and humiliation. My mother had never betrayed any fear of the white boys in khaki uniforms, who had carried impressive automatic rifles and sported ridiculously thick moustaches and Charles

Bronson-style sunglasses. Unlike Bronson, though, they carried real guns. These white men stood in stark contrast to Uncle Jimmy, the Portuguese man who owned our favourite fast-food shop back home.

They would rifle through my mother's luggage with their weapons and fling her petticoats and bras and my PJs out onto the road while the rest of the taxi passengers waited their turn. These border patrol officers seemed young – well, younger than my mother, whom I feared and respected and loved all at once. I never understood why those boys behaved the way they did, or where they got the balls to carry automatic rifles in my mother's presence. Or, more importantly, why their faces displayed such contempt for us.

It was at university that this inexplicable contempt started formulating itself into questions about race, power and social inequity. We sought political consciousness in the sweeping debris of student life in Braamfontein, a life punctuated by drunkenness and debauchery during the HIV scourge that threatened to snuff out our young lives with such indifference that we were forced to articulate the conditions of our fight for purpose and identity.

We had to confront, nakedly, our own blackness and the violence that aimed to destroy it. Instead of shrinking in horror from this insurmountable task, we chose to celebrate and explore it. In Braamfontein we began, in earnest, to play with things to which we'd had no access only a decade before. Having just missed the kwaito wave of Mdu's 'Tsiki-tsiki', Arthur Mafokate's 'Don't call me kaffir', Boom Shaka's 'It's about time', Joe Nina's 'Maria Podesta', Thebe's 'Tempy Life', Brothers of Peace and Crowded Crew, we slipped, quite deliberately, into American hip hop.

With hindsight, it seems a logical progression for us to have extended our tastes, in the early 2000s, to conscious black American hip-hop. Over there, they were free – seemingly just as we were – but, like us, not truly free. We dipped into Mos Def and Talib Kweli's album *Black Star*, Guru's *Jazzmatazz*, Public Enemy, Erykah Badu, Lauryn Hill and A Tribe Called Quest.

While the kwaito generation, of which we were a little part, liberated itself with every street bash, we were seeking ways to re-educate ourselves with hip hop records and books. We read Dambudzo Marechera's *House of Hunger* as a metaphor for our impoverished material condition and moral depravity. Tsitsi Dangarembga's *Nervous Conditions* hinted, for us, at the need for feminism and led us to question our privilege as young black men.

At Wits, we were suspicious of our white lecturers. We believed that they failed us intentionally, which we could never prove. We may have been free, but I couldn't help seeing, in every stare from a white person at Cresta Shopping Centre in Northcliff or The Waterfront (now Brightwater Commons) in Randburg, those boy soldiers and their Charles Bronson moustaches. Our white peers' contempt seemed to be lodged in something deeper than the politics of colour.

Clashes between black and white students in pubs in Arcadia and Hatfield in Pretoria gave us a sense of solidarity with students at the Pretoria Technikon (today, the Tshwane University of Technology) and the University of Pretoria. We may have made it into these hallowed institutions of higher learning, but we were still unwelcome. At Pretoria Technikon, The Heights student residence was reserved for black students – a Bantustan in a democratic South Africa.

We assumed, quite rightly, that this was a symptom of a system of structural domination in which we were the unwilling cogs, a manufactured underclass in perpetual service to a callous upper class despite our freedom. Still, we dreamt the dreams of our heroes – of a non-racial, non-sexist society in which we could live with the promise of equality.

We still dream, but the innocence of the promise of freedom is lost. Our former heroes have become potential adversaries, our former enemies likely allies.

As the fissures begin to show between the political class and the marginalised underclass, can we attest to a common, lived experience of the symbolic violence of the structural domination that defines class and race relations in South Africa? While the violence and inequality

66

stem from structural racial domination, further away at the margins this domination seems to express itself in the power play between those with relative privilege and those with none, regardless of race.

In my student days, we devoured Frantz Fanon and Steve Biko just as we read Michel Foucault and Pierre Bourdieu. We were as enamoured with Dumile Feni's art as with Claude Debussy's work.

We lived between the urban, the township and the rural – multiple realities at once. Some of us still do. These realities are forever shifting; at times, they appear not to be as black and white as one would like them to be.

Dying for equality

BRAD CIBANE

Today, black people – especially those of us who are still nursing apartheid wounds – are being blackmailed into accepting a distorted narrative of black resistance. It has become politically incorrect to speak of Nelson Mandela the militant freedom fighter. The ANC stalwart who, without trepidation, handed his freedom to the oppressor to help free the nation is being reduced to a monk who spent 27 years in prison meditating about peace.

The fervent leader of the mass resistance movement, the founder of the African National Congress's youth brigade, the strategist who helped depose formidable ANC President-General AB Xuma in 1949 and the first commander in chief of the revolutionary armed forces (the Spear of the Nation) has been turned into a campaigner for peace – an African Dalai Lama, if you will.

Mandela was part of the select group who founded the ANC Youth League, intended to become the 'brains-trust and power-station of the spirit of African nationalism', as the March 1944 Manifesto of the Youth League declared. The Manifesto further stated that 'Africans must struggle for development, progress and national liberation so as to occupy their rightful and honourable place among nations of the world'.

Yet today, the predominant narrative we face is one of nation-building and reconciliation, which renders the black struggle for equality and human dignity superfluous. In the context of the South African struggle for freedom and equality, endlessly courting reconciliation politics is misplaced.

Reconciliation assumes that there was conflict, what some call 'racial conflict'. However, South Africa has never experienced racial conflict, only oppressive domination on the basis of race. What South Africans needed then – and need now – is not peace and reconciliation, but freedom and equality.

Think about it: if one accepts that the struggle was about peace and unity, then the struggle is over, as we can ignore the remnants of centuries of economic exclusion, inferior education and land dispossession.

In 1946, after the government had killed twelve striking miners and wounded another 324, the ANC Youth League under Mandela's leadership declared that the 'mine workers' struggle is our struggle . . . we demand a living wage for all African workers!'

Is this struggle over?

In an article published by *Liberation* in 1956, Mandela declared that in 'demanding the nationalisation of the banks, the gold mines and the land the [Freedom] Charter strikes a fatal blow at the financial and gold-mining monopolies and farming interests that have for centuries plundered the country and condemned its people to servitude'. He went on to explain that such a step is imperative 'because the realisation of the Charter is inconceivable, in fact impossible, unless and until these monopolies are first smashed up and the national wealth of the country turned over to the people. The breaking up and democratisation of these monopolies will open up fresh fields for the development of a prosperous non-European bourgeois class.'

Have these objectives been achieved?

During his now-famed courtroom speech delivered from the dock in 1964, Mandela prophesied that '[the Freedom Charter] calls for redistribution, but not nationalisation, of land; it provides for nationalisation of mines, banks, and monopoly industry, because big monopolies are owned by one race only, and without such nationalisation racial domination would be perpetuated *despite the spread of political power*'.

During the same speech, Mandela went to great pains to explain that the struggle was about poverty and human dignity. He noted that whites enjoyed 'what may be the highest standard of living in the world, whilst Africans

70

live in poverty and misery. Poverty goes hand in hand with malnutrition and disease.' Once again, he declared that 'Africans want to be paid a living wage'.

More than 50 years later, Helen Zille, then still leader of the Democratic Alliance, took the opposite view when she wrote about the farmworkers' strike in the Western Cape in the party newsletter *SA Today*. 'As tough as it is to survive on the daily minimum wage, it is far tougher to earn nothing at all,' she says.

Zille goes on to explain that it is easy to see how 'the dominant (but entirely misleading) narrative arose of "heartless white farmers and labour brokers [who] make *super profits* by using *divide-and-rule* tactics to drive down workers' wages as their lives deteriorate"'. She dubs this narrative 'a stereotype'.

For as long as we allow the goal of the black struggle to be reduced to the ideal of peace and unity, Africans will continue to live in poverty. The status quo will persist and the black race will continue to be dominated by monopolists.

The black struggle has never been about race. Mandela said that political division on the basis of race is 'entirely artificial'. Instead, our struggle has been about the 'ideal of a democratic and free society in which all persons live together in harmony and with *equal opportunities*'.

It is for this ideal that Mandela was prepared to die.

---

* First published by the M&G's Thoughtleader

Seeing ourselves as we are

GCOBANI QAMBELA

Black unity: a term that rarely fits many black people's lived reality.

Angela Davis, political activist and scholar, made this claim in a talk in which she used the example of how, in the so-called black power movements in the US, 'black power' often denoted power for black men only, with there being no room for black women to participate. In her talk, Davis urged people to connect the struggle against racism to other struggles – especially those against discrimination based on gender, sexuality, class and so on. Achille Mbembe, who introduced Davis, observed that one of the most important lessons to learn from Davis is to avoid theorising without keeping in touch with praxis: we should see ourselves as we are, and not as we ought to be.

I was reminded of Davis's talk when I read an article by commentator and writer Khaya Dlanga in the *Mail & Guardian.* In his article, Dlanga laments people's responses to the #blackface controversy at the University of Pretoria in August 2014. 'You would think that someone who goes to university, like the two students who dressed in blackface, would be self-aware and knowledgeable enough to understand that certain things are just unacceptable,' Dlanga writes.

What interested me about Dlanga's article was not his analysis of the blackface incident, but rather the ways in which it showed how many black men still cannot connect the struggle against racism to broader struggles against other forms of discrimination. While it seems, at first glance, that Dlanga opposes racism in general, a closer inspection of his work – his praxis – reveals a black man deeply committed to anti-black racism that privileges black men primarily.

In another column, about interracial relationships, Dlanga shares a story about a black male friend who asked him to write a column. Dlanga's friend found it notable that he had ended up dating white women as he had struggled 'to get with black women in South Africa because he sense[d] a barrier' – not being South African, and having attended elite schools that limited his exposure to other black people, he spoke no indigenous South African languages.

Dlanga writes about how his friend had not been able to crack 'the black code'. To remedy this, Dlanga took it upon himself to teach his friend black phrases such as 'towning', 'yellow bone', and *'eziwey'*. 'Towning' means having sex without a condom; *'eziwey'* is a derogatory term that refers to women as 'these things'; and 'yellow bone' is a term referring to light-skinned black people. This term plays into colourism politics by treating people of the same race differently based solely on their skin colour. As Yaba Amgborale Blay notes, 'colourism constructs a spectrum upon which individuals attempt to circumnavigate the parameters of the white/non-white binary racial hierarchy by instead assigning and assuming colour privilege based upon proximity to Whiteness'.

I was shocked: Dlanga is under the impression that accessing the so-called black code to date black women involved misogynoir – misogyny directed at black women. The terms that his column claims he taught his friend are unacceptable.

In a country like South Africa, where HIV affects black women most severely, it is simply irresponsible to use words like 'towning' – this term contains its own unspeakable violence. And 'yellow bone', like 'blackface', is deeply wounding. It is directly tied to, and embedded in, colonialism and the way in which it dehumanised black people. In their book *African Masculinities: Men in Africa from the Late Nineteenth Century to the Present*, Lahoucine Ouzgane and Robert Morrell note that European historians, drawing on earlier work of ethnologists, glorified the achievements of the Egyptians 'while tacitly or explicitly negating the history of non-Egyptians'. They note that one way of doing this was 'to develop derogatory terms for peoples deemed to have been part of ancient civilisations. Another way was to credit lighter-skinned inhabitants of the continent with more intelligence than darker-skinned people and to attribute to them the credit for African civilisation.'

In *Black Looks: Race and Representation*, bell hooks writes about the direct links between the persistence of white supremacist patriarchy and the institutionalisation of certain representations of blackness 'that support and maintain the oppression, exploitation, and overall domination of all black people'.

We should be very careful not to use public platforms to denigrate black women – and equally aware that we cannot disentangle sexism from racism.

Beyond racism

KOKETSO MOETI

The idea of South Africa as a rainbow nation is a myth that some still hold dear, even though it has slowly but surely lost all credibility. Moot see it, now, for what it really is: the illusion that 21 years of democracy can undo over 350 years of oppression and hatred.

South Africans, unfortunately, have a penchant for political correctness. Consequently, in some company race and racism have become difficult – or even taboo – topics, even though our history as a nation cannot be separated from them.

We can't move beyond racism without discourse about it.

In this sense, those involved in the racist diatribes against the Rhodes Must Fall collective have done the nation a favour. Their reactions – pictures of monkeys replacing the fallen statue of Cecil John Rhodes, of monkeys eating their own shit, the use of the word k****r, and many more – were honest, at least. They saw to it that the battle lines were drawn and drew real responses, not the politically correct bullshit we are used to hearing.

In this reaction, it was fascinating to see – as Gillian Schutte eloquently describes in an article entitled 'The Whiteness Smorgasbord' – how 'whiteness is often presented as victim to the "savagery" of blackness in the form of endless whinging [*sic*] about crime, corruption, inefficiency and BEE'. I can only agree with her when she writes that 'from intellectual discourse, to mainstream chatter, to barely educated braai banter, whiteness is always sure of one thing – superiority over other races – particularly the African race. Whether it is disguised in liberal equanimity or downright racism, this whiteness discourse espouses the same learnt notion that white is right – even in a so-called Rainbow Nation.'

Of course, these racist diatribes were widely condemned by both black and white. However, there was more outrage about the use of the word 'k****r' and the pictures of monkeys than about the matter of institutional racism and other forms of oppression that the collective was raising. That black people are still referred to as k****rs is evidenced on a variety of social media platforms: in the erstwhile News24 comments, on the *3rd Degree* Facebook page and in the way some white folk say 'your government' to black people, despite that government also being theirs.

How do words that people claim they never use find themselves in people's vocabulary when they are in a state of heightened emotion? By being used, no doubt, around dinner tables, on farms, in schools and on campuses – even by members of the born-free generation. The only conclusion one can draw is that these people's referring to black people as African monkeys and k****rs is common, and that these words are used in the presence of others, who have clearly condoned their use. Why else would they think it is appropriate to say such racist hogwash in public?

When caught out, some people apologise, even if forced to do so by a Chapter 9 institution; they always seem to have an excuse for having used the word in the first place.

Those who are sympathetic to racists make comments about how black people should 'get over it', and that k****r 'is just a word'. There may even be discussions about where the word originated and what it means, all of which I strongly believe are misguided. Origins be damned – in South Africa that word was, and is, used to degrade, oppress and dehumanise.

Those who feel that people have come down too heavily on these racists seem to overlook the fact that South Africa's poverty and deep-rooted inequality are a direct consequence of apartheid. We seem to forget that apartheid was not merely a phenomenon of racial hatred – it was also a deeply entrenched system of racial domination that affected every facet of life in South Africa. It led to the deliberate underdevelopment of black communities, the dispossession of people from their land and, in turn, from housing, and discrimination in the quality of basic rights and services, including health care, education and social security. It's going to take a long time to undo the legacy of apartheid.

Despite everything that has been achieved in the past 21 years, the reality is that we still have two education systems and two health-care systems, for example. It is often argued that black people have full access to all the privileges that were once reserved for white people, but this is misleading: the majority of black people cannot afford these services. The Whites Only signs may have been removed, but black South Africans still face barriers.

It is easy for those who have benefited from the privilege that came with apartheid to condone such thinking. They may even claim that their attitude is justifiable because black people sing *Dubula Ibhunu*. South Africans who have ended up privileged today, despite the past, are often blind to the suffering of our people.

On public forums, we preach the rainbow nation – but it's going to take a whole lot more than the removal of Whites Only signs to undo apartheid's damage and hurt. Many people want neither to hear nor accept this fact. Until we speak openly about this truth, we cannot pave the way; people will continue to be 'shocked' and 'appalled' by manifestations of the racism that lurks just below the surface of our precious rainbow nation.

Chasing white elephants

NOMSA MAZWAI

Given our dire need for infrastructure, why are so many white elephants strewn not only over the Eastern Cape but also the country? This is my story – one that illustrates, sadly, that a vacuum of leadership and consciousness ensures that in South Africa, even the most hopeful of interventions – with experts at the helm – so often end up as white elephants.

A few years ago, after I'd graduated from the University of Fort Hare with an honours degree in Economics, a visionary named Phila Xuza employed me as a project officer at her organisation – Aspire, the Economic Development Agency for the Eastern Cape's Amathole district. Phila taught me the virtue of hard work; here, I began my journey with what would later become my passion: Emthonjeni Arts, formerly known as the Hamburg Artists' Retreat.

The project was one of many anchor projects engineered

to regenerate the economies of small towns in rural areas, economic growth and development that would, in turn, create new opportunities for those in the hinterland. Whereas Aspire worked primarily in the Amathole district, it wished to answer one of South Africa's biggest problems: how to empower and uplift rural communities. These communities make up the majority of our country, yet funds earmarked for their development seldom extend beyond social grants and activities that build dependence on the state.

Fresh out of graduate school, my eyes opened to the growth potential of the rural poor. I felt that creating opportunities in rural areas would help to address issues of urban migration – that rural South Africans were more than just cheap labour and poverty statistics.

The project required passion, creativity and a commitment to the country. Ordinary South Africans, trying to address the challenges of poverty and an inaccessible economy, donated services like the design of the building – a structure that would take five years to build at a cost R35 million. When funds were allocated and the project kicked off, those of us involved with the project were overwhelmed with possibility and achievement. In a community that had never believed that this could happen, expectations suddenly became very real; people on the ground, many of whom were disillusioned with the government, once again started to believe.

Before construction began, I was awarded a Fulbright scholarship and went to the US to do my Masters. On my return, I was delighted to discover that the retreat, now named Emthonjeni Arts, was looking for a management team. I applied for the post of Director, which I was awarded after two gruelling interviews. I had a clear under-standing of the project, the approach, its intentions and its aspirations. It was more than just a building to me. I believed in it: the project, the dream, the community.

After my appointment in late 2012, I began plotting a way forward with the project's first managers, but also with the community and stakeholders – keeping in mind that we had to be global in our thinking and operations, ensuring our relevance on a global scale as an inter-national artist's residency, but that we'd always need to strive to create local development opportunities.

Despite delays in appointments and demands from our funders to meet the milestones set out in the business plan, we hit the ground running. A team of proud South Africans, we put our backs into it; this was a calling, not a job.

About three months in, there were two big changes in our stakeholder landscape: the appointment of a new Aspire CEO, and of a new acting municipal manager of the local municipality. Emthonjeni perplexed both women. They had no clear understanding of its foundations, but did have a clear idea of what they thought the organisation was supposed to be doing – an idea that was not in the business plan.

It happens often in South Africa. We start with a plan. We research it, test it, start rolling it out. Initially, we are happy with progress. During construction, employment levels are high; people are busy, and progress is tangible. Once construction is complete, progress slows perceptibly. Trucks may come and go, dropping off equipment; soon, there is nothing more to deliver. Managing expectations becomes critical, for which communication of a clear plan is central. Having worked with communitioo before, we ensured that we scheduled a time, once a month, to report back to the community in the local language on progress and to gather their input. It was a participatory process.

In this sector, you can dot every 'i' and cross every 't', but you need, always, to be ready for surprises. Because the new Aspire CEO and acting municipal manager believed that the project should have gone to tender, we were to face our biggest unanticipated challenge.

Despite Aspire and the municipality having been involved in construction on every step of the way, they now felt we had no right to exist.

It started with insults and suggestions that we were incompetent, running the organisation poorly. Neither of the new appointees had read the business plan, nor did they have the background to understand the project's origin and destination. Not that they were interested: on multiple occasions, while trying to explain the basis upon which the intervention was formulated – that it was one project, part of a regional approach – we were shut down and threatened with legal action. That ours was one of many other interventions in the Amathole region suddenly became immaterial.

For the next six months, Aspire bottlenecked our funding and refused to recognise the project's management team or board, alleging that we had been appointed illegally and that the organisation was unlawful. Their view was that a private operator should have been receiving subsidy funding to run the project – this despite our progress on site; indicators that suggested that our approach to local development was working; synergy among projects; and acceptance of and involvement by local communities. Our achievements were worth celebrating, yet we'd become Aspire and the local municipality's problem child.

How had this happened?

On multiple occasions, I'd found myself paying portions of payroll to keep the project going through what I knew was a storm that would soon be over. On paper, the business was no longer viable; layers of red tape were smothering the passion, the community was becoming restless, and a service delivery strike was looming.

Maintenance that required anything more than the tools

we had and our in-house handyman was shelved. Before long, the building – like the dream – began to fall apart. It did so not only because we had no funds for proper maintenance, but also because, I believe, the contractors had deliberately built a white elephant. Having built so many before, they cut corners that they assumed would never be discovered before the structure fell into disuse.

The septic tank could not handle the waste produced by staff and two on-site managers, less than 20 per cent of the building's capacity.

The paint was so watered down that when the rainy season came, it simply washed off.

All the looks were different, glaringly obvious leftovers from other projects.

The building had the most unbelievable leaks: I'm talking waterfalls in some of the rooms. The leak in my office was so bad that I could have showered in it.

So: the municipality was dead set on taking over the facility. What they were going to do with it was clear not even to them. The development agency, having changed leadership, had metamorphosed into a quasi-legal firm or policy unit. The architects were dodging the bullets of their contractual obligations, knowing full well they'd never be brought to task. Had someone tried to, redeployments or leadership changes would have confused them clean out of the line of fire.

I tried to keep my wits about me, to remember the virtues of perseverance I'd been taught at school. But every day, it became harder to face my staff, to sell what I now knew was a lie.

Here, at the edge of self-loathing and failure, I wonder: Is this how people lose hope? Lose their being, and become disillusioned about their country? How the strong are broken? Despite standing strong, I realise that a lot has broken inside me.

As soon as a white elephant is built, the advert about what the government and the private sector are doing for you is over; we return to the horror of South African life. A life in which, at the start of each new project, someone shouts 'action'. The camera starts rolling, bricks are laid, ribbons are tied, officials are called. Ribbons are cut, which is what the director shouts.

Only, some of us don't hear him. We begin to work, to give life to the set we'd built. Slowly, we discover that the set is just that – a production whose extras are real people on the ground, people who have been betrayed by their government.

There is an even bigger elephant at play here than the white elephant in my story. It's the elephant in the room: the problem of nations on the African continent. Why are we all so ill fated? Could it be that our leaders are all ruthless and greedy, or could it be something else? DStv? America? Democracy?

I believe it's because of our lack of substance. As a young person growing up in South Africa, I think we lack substance: consciousness, self-knowledge, an understanding where we come from and, consequently, an inability to fathom a future, an idea of where we are going as a collective. Our president is colouring between the lines, taking the most he can from his position. After all, he has no plan for a sustainable future; if he had, he would have made sustainable long-term choices like keeping Thabo Mbeki in office till the end of his term, even if it were just for show. That choice would have kept our country stable, built confidence in our institutions, and made the world imagine a different African narrative.

But we should not despair. We face challenges – many challenges – but we should never stop trying to build the South Africa and Africa that many of us believe is possible. We define our destiny.

To this end, I continue to communicate regularly with my community. I keep them informed about the project, what we are doing and where we hope to go with it. We pay close attention to what the community needs; being responsive to these needs keeps us relevant. I think about the good people, doing good things, who never make the news – the officials who work tirelessly to ensure that this flame is not snuffed.

Apartheid took decades to build. Ubuntu – the original

system of love, empowerment and respect – will take time, too. Yet the choice is not ours to make. So, we roll up our sleeves every morning, and work towards realising the dream of real freedom for our people.

I'll do it. Even though it feels like I'm chasing white elephants.

Who am I to quit, when my forefathers and foremothers died trying?

3

Romance in the time of freedom

Mergers and aqcuisitions
OWETHU KHELI

Have you seen that clever booze ad whose last line claims that in the olden days, mergers and acquisitions were not negotiated by lawyers? What a load of bull.

I have just gone through a merger – or an acquisition, or perhaps both – of my own. Yes, I am talking about lobola negotiations, the deal that will link me, my fiancée and our families for good. What an exciting stage. And a painful one – I knew it was going to leave a gaping hole in my wallet.

Tradition dictates that the bride's family gives the groom's family a hard time during the negotiations. So, my team included 'lawyers' who, fortunately, did not realise that they were lawyers or they would have charged me accordingly.

As a Xhosa man, there are two certainties in life: you will be circumcised and you will pay lobola. I'd actually started saving for lobola when I was 21 – but a couple of years later I'd blown the money when I'd decided to buy property before saying 'I do'.

At 30, it was time for me to do the right thing. I knew my dad had been itching for a while to play the role of briefing attorney. I called him up: 'Are you ready?'

He didn't hesitate for a moment, and rounded up two of his cousins to be the 'advocates'. We got into the car the following week and crossed the Kei Bridge in the Eastern Cape for Mthatha, to meet the opposing team's 'lawyers' – my fiancée's dad and company.

I was not allowed into the house in which my lawyers and my future father-in-law discussed the terms of this 'out-of-court settlement' – my presence would have been contempt of court. The lawyers – known in isiXhosa as *oonozakuzaku* – deal, of course, in cattle. My fiancée's family would say how many cattle they wanted for her, and attach a monetary value to each cow. It was my lawyers' duty to knock down both the number of cows and the value of each one. In the end, it would take three meetings for the two families to come to an agreement.

The first meeting, according to my team's debriefing, was a good one. 'It's a smooth process,' said my dad's cousin.

'Okay,' I said, 'tell me more.'

According to him, my fiancée's family had accepted our merger-of-equals proposition. Wait, did I hear a 'but' in his voice? Indeed. The opposing team had not done due

94

diligence and could not put cattle or a monetary value on the daughter, he explained.

What? After arranging the meeting well in advance and travelling all the way to Mthatha, they weren't ready? *Uh . . . these people are playing games*, I thought.

All I wanted to know was how many thousands I would have to part with. I wanted an easy deal: a reasonable lobola, then my family and I would pay for the wedding. My lawyers claimed that they suggested this to her family. Either my darling's family was not that keen, or they did not realise how sweet a deal that would be for them.

They played hard to get over those three meetings, my team informed me. At one stage, I considered going to the house next door to find a wife instead. Or marrying a white woman, whose dad would have the pain of funding a lavish wedding with no lobola.

Finally, the deal was sealed in the most welcome and fulfilling of ways. I sneaked into the final meeting. You see, my lawyers are rebels – they tend to break tradition. They said I should walk in with them to experience the process for myself.

The opposing team did not miss this and probed masterfully, as though they did not know who I was. One of them subtly asked, 'Gentlemen, how come there are four of you when in previous meetings there were only three?'

My dad's cousin, knowing we could be fined, introduced me as their driver. Everybody laughed.

The modern Xhosa man in me does not question the value of lobola. It is one of the pillars that should hold two families – and, especially, a couple – together. Whenever I feel like throwing a tantrum during disagreements with my fiancée, I quickly remind myself that there is more at stake than just my ego.

My lawyers had worked hard for this deal. It is now for me to enjoy it, not to go and spoil it.

* This piece was first published in the *Mail & Guardian*.

First contact

VANGILE GANTSHO

In a recent taxi ride from Randburg to Braamfontein, I found myself surprisingly charmed by the taxi driver. He quoted poetry (Mzwakhe Mbuli) and songs (Dionne Farris), was delightful to all the passengers and was, at times, genuinely funny.

Most importantly, he found a way to make me feel really special. Granted, his taxi industry references were lost on me – there was a lot of polite smiling – but I must admit that his was one of the most pleasant taxi rides I'd had in a long time.

He didn't even ask for my number afterwards. All he said was that I should remember that I am beautiful and carry myself as such. (I know, right?)

The thing is, when I got home and told a friend about him, she laughed at me (or him? I'm not quite sure), then immediately dismissed my experience as part of my fascination with people. Apparently, there are certain lines within the dating pool that not only become more apparent as we grow older, but should also not be crossed.

It's true, I thought. At varsity you could meet someone while you were waitressing and even date him for some time, because you shared a space. However, the minute one of you graduated and it became more apparent that, for example, one was paying his or her way through school and the other had career-waiter aspirations, things would go horribly wrong.

These social, economic and cultural lines are drawn in the wind and adhered to silently, with very few lovers venturing beyond them for fear of unnecessary complications. What happened to 'I'm just a girl, standing in front of a boy, asking him to love me'?

In my quest to understand why my friend had laughed so hard (and why I knew, in the back of my mind, that I'd been more entertained than charmed), I did some research: I asked a few friends whether they would date below their income bracket. More specifically, I asked whether any jobs were no-go dating areas for them.

It was interesting to note the clear split in the responses I got. In general, many people felt that they would date people who had the same socio-economic aspirations and led similar lifestyles – provided these people had good hearts, were socially responsible and met all those 'beautiful pancreas' (inner beauty) requirements, of course.

Many of my artistic friends felt that a potential partner's

cultural, emotional and spiritual characteristics were more important than the jobs they did, but later admitted that on first contact (especially if there was a uniform involved) they would probably say no.

My professional – and I use this word with caution – friends were a lot more straightforward. 'No. Taxi drivers, petrol attendants, security guards and generally all unskilled workers are a no-go for me,' one 30-year-old financial services professional told me.

What was interesting was that no one wanted to date a person whose goal was, say, to be a petrol attendant. Potential could still be negotiated up to a certain age, but it was very clear that most people would only consider a partner with an unskilled job if there was a compelling reason for him or her being in that position. Said job had to be a means to an end, and not the final destination.

Another friend said she needed to know whether the person had dreams and aspirations: 'Because you can become a police commissioner or a bank manager through internal structures. A security guard, on the other hand, I can't consider. Why aren't they a cop, with health cover and life insurance? It depends, but if they don't have dreams and ambitions, then no. And a definite no to a security guard.'

When you think about it, a CEO of a multimillion-rand organisation is rarely found dating a security guard, especially if that CEO is a woman. As a friend so eloquently put it, 'Such situations only work out in Tyler Perry movies.' This brings another reality of the dating game into the argument: in the real world, it would appear that successful men are more willing to overlook their partners' professions in favour of other attributes than successful women.

I soon realised that each of us walks into a relationship with a set of negotiables and non-negotiables. Some are financial; others are social, cultural, emotional, intellectual or spiritual. In the wise words of Mam'G (my mom), '*Uthando lubalulekile mntana'm, nencoko funeka idibane, kodwa indlala xa ingena ngomnyango, uthando luphuma nge festile* (Love is important, my child, and the conversation must flow, but when poverty comes through the door, love climbs out the window).'

As much as we all want to be good people and give good people a chance, the truth of the matter is that the work we do is a major part of the people we become. As charming as the taxi driver was, his work made elements of him undesirable to me; I would have preferred it if someone else had made me feel special.

A preference, not a prejudice.

* For interest's sake, the top five undesirable jobs for partners according to my survey are:
  1. Taxi driver
  2. Security guard

3. Petrol attendant
4. Truck driver
5. Prison warder.

Confessions of a sub

TSHEGOFATSO SENNE

So – a little over two years ago, I discovered BDSM (bondage and discipline/sadism and masochism).

I had spent years contemplating that little corner of my mind that had always been curious about white women in spandex and leather who wielded crops and whips and tied men up against the walls of dark dungeons. It intrigued and terrified me in equal measure. That's the impression most people have of BDSM, right?

Little did I know . . .

It was only when I started having sex regularly that I began to investigate BDSM – watching, reading, asking questions, exploring. I was lucky enough to be with a partner who was well aware of how exploratory I was; together, we created a safe space in which I could question why and how I enjoyed sex – the things I loved doing, and those that made my toes curl. Out of true hedonistic curiosity, I sought out more things to bring me pleasure.

As I began my journey into The Life, I read up on spanking and choking, name-calling and humiliation, and all the things that now make me swoon. After getting onto Twitter and starting to interact with black kinksters (What? I thought this shit was for white people?), I fell even more deeply in love with the part of my life that often left me bruised and smiling.

I had never felt so comfortable with my body and the things it wanted until I started exploring kink. I learnt from other people, absorbing everything I could. I had never felt so happy with my thoughts, and felt even happier that I'd begun to feel comfortable with verbalising them after years of thinking, *Jeez, Tshego, your mind is disgusting*. I relished the thought of masturbating and was affirmed every time I could guide someone to lead me to orgasm; I knew what my body liked.

I laughed at the people who called me a slut, and savoured watching their faces collapse when I agreed with a smile. Man! When I speak of kink, I speak of it with such love that most people get confused: they have one idea in their minds, and I another. So, usually, conversations about kink involve me explaining my own experience of it and informing others about the elements of complete vulnerability and romance that you won't find in the Bondage tag on Pornhub.

I would talk about sex and kink all day if I could, as most people who follow me on Twitter will attest. It's great to see how interested people get when I explain that I'm submissive. I especially enjoy their confusion: I supposedly give off dominant vibes. Whereas I am exploring my switch side – the side that is able to enjoy being both dominant and submissive – I adore being a sub.

On that note, being a sub is fucking difficult. Holy hell – the people in the know don't tell you this. What they do tell you is that you're strong and in control, and that nothing will happen if you don't want it to. The knowledge that you can retain control by handing it over to someone else is an amazing thought – and feeling, once you get into it. But what they don't tell you is that an internal crisis often comes with the introspection and constant self-evaluation that hides in the corner of the pretty bag that holds your attempts to process these strengths – these limits to your consent. It is all about boundaries and the ways in which you allow someone else to cross them. You would never have felt comfortable allowing this boundary-crossing until you'd met someone who seems to take better care of you than you take of yourself.

They forget to tell you that part and parcel of this is having the strength to hand over your insecurities and have someone cater to them in a way that cradles you so warmly that you feel displaced when they leave. They don't tell you about the effect that admitting things about yourself that you aren't comfortable with outside your position as a sub will have, and that these admissions may haunt you and your future relationships. Initially, you can't quite articulate it.

They also don't tell you that this strength is what allows you to become a baby who sputters and sobs without worrying about seeming weak. They don't tell you how good it feels when your tears dry and someone calls you 'my baby' – like you're being cradled in the warmest part of the most genuine smile you've ever seen.

The sides of BDSM that few people speak about (maybe this is my ignorance speaking – let's rather say the sides of BDSM that I haven't heard or read much about) are the ones I hold closest to my heart and share the least – experiences that go way beyond the scope of leather and spanking, and that give you just as much pleasure but without physical touch. They make me wish that everyone could find and swoon in their own brand of romance.

Of course, the recent *Fifty Shades of Grey* obsession had many people out there believing that BDSM is for them. No problem, right? Wrong. It's not only annoying that being a sub is now associated with that badly written book that's soaked in abuse, but it targets people who are going through what we call a sub frenzy.

Once people realise that they may be a sub, they tend to go on a rampage to find a dom. I went through this, too; obviously, I wanted to get into it as quickly as possible, to learn and feel as much as I could. Putting yourself in harm's way by making yourself vulnerable to someone who doesn't know what the fuck they're doing, however, is a problem – one that becomes serious when the person to whom you relinquish control cares more about his or her pleasure than your comfort.

All the good things I've described? Yeah, that shit isn't possible when one of you is desperate to learn and the other takes advantage of that.

When you enter a D/S dynamic, you have to learn as much as you can about the inner workings of the kink. It takes a lot to reach the point of handing over your body and mind and allowing an outside influence to lead you in a way that you hope is good for you.

It's really difficult. I keep saying it: maybe it's because I'm sensitive and get hurt easily; maybe it's because I'm a hard-ass and find handing trust over incredibly difficult. Either way, I want people who are interested in kink to be safe about it. I want people to be able to explore without being coerced or taken advantage of or hurt. In a nutshell, I want people to have the sex and get the love they deserve.

These are some of the things that have been on my mind for some time. I'm no expert – everything I share links back to my personal experience, which is why I love to hear how others experience kink. My Twitter account, blog and weekly column are there for clarification, greater understanding and questions, so drop me a line.

I don't bite unless I'm asked to.

Playing the dating game

YOLISA QUNTA

I am dating, currently, with a purpose: to find a husband. This makes dating slightly different from the times I've dated out of sheer boredom, habit, or the simple desire to change my Facebook status.

There is usually no middle ground with my dates: either I'm in a Puff Daddy video, or it's so bad I'd prefer to die alone, surrounded by cats. When it's good, it's good – helicopter rides, bottomless champagne, shopping sprees to work up an appetite, swanning around in five-star hotels. Once, a generous man from Johannesburg even lent me his overpriced SUV for six months so I could 'see what it felt like'. When it's bad, it's sitting in Fontana on Long Street wondering how fast food constitutes a date, or shivering on a windy beach and eating mouthfuls of sand with soggy sandwiches. Whoever told homeboy that sunset picnics were romantic forgot to add that the romance factor was entirely weather dependent.

Strange individuals with strange habits have crossed my path. Dating in these times can be a minefield – many of the old rules no longer apply, and new standards haven't been laid down yet. This is why dating, for me, has been a happy mix of good times and awkward encounters. I have survived the bad times by choosing to turn the horrors into stories to amuse my friends; the more painful memories I have erased with white wine.

However, I am still left with a few questions. To empower myself with all the resources I'll need to find my soul mate, future husband and father of my children, they need answering.

1. What's up, Mr Chatty?

A year or two ago, I dated two train wrecks in succession – let's call them Piggy and Loser. I didn't lick my wounds for very long. When I decided I was ready to dive back into the dating pool, I discovered the joys of internet dating. A whole new world opened up for me.

The first question that most guys ask online is, 'Do you have WhatsApp?' I'm not an early adopter when it comes to technology, but even I was using it by then, thinking it a handy way to communicate with friends and family members who didn't insist that I join their WhatsApp groups.

Being fresh on the scene, I made the mistake of giving my number to a few guys immediately after meeting online. I soon realised that most had little or no intention of ever meeting. They just wanted to chat for hours on end.

About the most banal stuff.

WhatsApp also opens the door for losers who nag for photos. I asked one guy why he needed more photos of me when he had seen numerous pictures on the dating site, as well as my WhatsApp avatar. His response? He didn't know how old the photos were and 'just needed to check' that I still looked the same.

Charmer.

Talk is cheap. Now, I'll only give out my number on the day of the date to smooth out logistics.

2. Why do u typ lyk ths?

Of all the things that irk me about dating in the 21st century, this one tops the list. Nothing makes me go from intrigued to indifferent than a grown man who texts like a teenager.

Let's take the example of Kwezi, who hailed from Zambia and was doing a master's degree at a Cape Town university. Kwezi was ridiculously good looking. I'm talking fine like Morris Chestnut in his prime, with a body like a Zulu god.

Our first date was a group excursion with friends to entertainment park Ratanga Junction. He arrived on time, brought Lindt chocolate and took my friend's kid on the teacup ride so we could do all the scary ones. So far, so fine.

When he dropped me off, I waited a few hours before sending a kind 'I had a good time' message. What did I get in response? A message that looked like it had been typed by someone who was being charged R100 for every vowel.

The time I have to spend deciphering these messages annoys my inner grumpy old lady. I'm okay with the basics like 'l8tr', but 'wud' for 'what are you doing'? At this point, all I could think about was Edvard Munch's *The Scream*.

I went from dreaming up names for our kids to completely uninterested in two seconds flat. My married friend chided me for being shallow. I struggled to explain that, in my mind, 'writng lyk ths' is something only kids do.

In the interests of educating myself, however, I asked a few guys why they do this. Here are some of the responses I've had so far:

- It's more convenient for me because it's quicker.
- Everyone else does it.
- I only type full words when I'm communicating professionally. I'm not at work, so it's okay.

In all of my enquiries, I got the subtle message that I was the problem, forcing people to do onerous things like type full words and complete sentences. Really? I'm sorry, but if you find yourself unable to go to the trouble of using proper grammar when communicating with me, don't expect me to go to the trouble of pitching up for our next date.

3. On a perfect first date, who foots the bill?

When it comes to dating, I'm like the United Nations: I believe the world is bursting with goodness in all sorts of nationalities. I've gone on dates with men from all over the planet. Some, I suspect, were from outer space. I've also concluded that, given half a chance, men from all over the world are equally capable of jaw-dropping acts of rudeness.

I once went on a first date with a Spanish guy who was a professor of Astrophysics at UCT. He offered to name a black hole after me, stayed for exactly one drink, then left, claiming he had prior arrangements with his friends. The genius texted me a week later, asking why I hadn't kissed him after the date and when we'd be going out again.

Then there was the Dubai-born financier who told me that I looked very sexy in my pictures and that he'd been waiting all night for me to pounce on him.

But of all the rudeness I've encountered, South African men are the only ones who think it is perfectly normal to ask you out, enjoy a great meal, drink themselves jolly and then, when the bill comes, to look you in the eye and say, 'You're going to take care of this, right?'

I'm not violently opposed to the idea of a woman paying for a date – if she has offered to, or if it's a special occasion and you're treating your boo thang. By all means, whip out your plastic and do the right thing. But if a man asks me out on a date, I fully expect him to pay. When we've become a steady item, we can look at going Dutch or whatever works best for our mutual finances. But if you try to leave me with the bill on one of our first dates, you know for sure it will be the last time we'll be seeing each other.

Not all South African men have short arms and long pockets, but in my experience they are the only ones who think that saddling their date with the bill is acceptable behaviour. To add insult to injury, some still have the nerve to chirp about how they admire independent women – as if it's a compliment and not a way to manipulate you into paying for dinner. For those not familiar with pop culture, Beyoncé fired everyone in Destiny's Child who tried to get in the way of her rise to the top, because *that* is what independent women do. They get rid of problematic individuals. Quickly.

During the #findahusband search, I will continue to date across nationalities. I will even date South African men. But the next time there is a shortfall, someone is going to end up doing the dishes. And it's not going to be the pretty one with the manicure.

4. Who asked you for your dick pic?

As a sexually active heterosexual woman, I genuinely have no problem with penises. But I also believe that this part of the male anatomy is a matter of function over form.

Penises are delightful, and infinitely entertaining, but not very pretty to look at. Especially when pictures of them are unsolicited.

I understand that some couples exchange racy pictures to keep it spicy, or whatever. However, I have never sent a text saying, 'Please can I see your private parts?' I have received a few pictures of men's nether regions nonetheless.

Sometimes there is not even a preamble. I joined a random Facebook group once. One of the other members sent me an inbox message saying 'Hi', accompanied by a smiley face. I didn't respond. Two days later, I got another message – a full frontal.

In the beginning I was shocked, offended and, sometimes, slightly amused by these unwanted images. Now I forward the images to the offender via e-mail and copy some of his acquaintances in. I let him know that I find this behaviour unacceptable and that if it happens again, I will share the pictures with his boss and colleagues. (In the case of my Facebook 'friend', I posted the photo to his timeline and asked him why he thought it appropriate to send it to me.)

This seems to take care of the problem.

5. When you talk trash about your ex, do you think it impresses me?

I understand that by the time you get to a certain age,

your dating history includes the good, the bad and the ugly. There is definitely a time and place to vent about the evil person who broke your heart, then poured acid into the cavity in your chest. In the comfort of your own home, mostly, ugly-crying to Adele and eating ice cream straight from the tub.

Since my life is for your entertainment, I had dinner, recently, with a guy I'd been out with a few times before. He felt comfortable enough to launch into a lengthy story about why his ex was a 'psycho bitch'. I'm partial to a few choice swear words if the occasion calls for it, but using misogynistic language over Caprese salad on our third date is not the wave.

I tried to explain why, as a woman, I found the word offensive and that, as the father of a twelve-year-old girl, he was not setting a good example. I also pointed out that since he did not have a medical degree, he was not qualified to diagnose another human being's mental state. He stared at me as if I was the crazy person.

Tip of the day: If you speak to a potential new partner about your ex in derogatory terms, she will correctly assume that that is how you will talk about her should you break up. It's a romance killer. Don't go there.

6. Does your mother know you act like this?

About all of the above. Asking for a friend.

One would think that these are basic things, but judging by the rudeness that passes for standard dating etiquette these days, there is clearly a knowledge gap. In short, some of the single men I've met along the way have made me think that a dating guide would not be wasted on most of them. Nothing as icky as the techniques espoused by the author of *The Game*; it's just that a few pointers on how to behave could significantly increase your chances of a second date.

4

Seeking enlightenment

An untold history lesson

SONGEZO MABECE

I have spent a good two hours writing this exam paper and am relieved finally to be constructing a good response, with just over an hour to go before pens down. No later than my relief comes, the intercom rings and, with that, my answer vanishes.

'The school is requested to please stop writing, stand at attention and observe a moment's silence in honour of Armistice Day. The *Reveille* and the *Last Post* will sound. Teachers are reminded to please give pupils an extra fifteen minutes of writing time. Thank you.'

The resultant silence was broken by the sound of trumpets as the *Last Post* and *Reveille* filtered into my receptive ears. Those who know their history will know that this is generally what was being observed throughout the Commonwealth: a truly British tradition on the eleventh of the eleventh, at eleven. To this day, red poppies are worn in honour of Remembrance Day. For what it is worth, the British are to be lauded for the manner in which their fallen are immortalised.

But what does that mean for Songezo Mabece? Of what relevance is Remembrance Day for him as a young man, whose root and stem is deeply embedded in the Afrikan soil?

This war was fought at a time when my forefathers were fourth-class citizens in their ancestral home. Their class followed, in ascending order of privilege, that of the Coloured, Indian and white person. At this time (and since long before), my forefathers were fighting wars of their own – against the settler citizen, in the main. In what is now the Eastern Cape (formerly part of the Cape Colony), there is an area referred to as Frontier Country – the span where some of these wars were fought. Fort Beaufort, Fort Cox, Fort Fordyce and Fort Hare, among others, are station names that are synonymous with the region. Chiefs and warriors in the form of Ndlambe, Maqoma, and Nxele (Makana) et al. were their adversaries. From these military contests, towns like Grahamstown, Port Elizabeth, Alice, King Williams Town and others were founded following the conquest of the rifle in what has become known as the 100-Year War.

Then there was the colossal Zulu leader, King Shaka. He is unarguably one of the greatest Afrikan leaders. His territory played host to one of the most crushing defeats suffered by the British, at the hands of the Zulu nation –

the Battle of Isandlwana. I could even talk about the tribal wars and battles that plagued (within and without) the indigenous Afrikan language groups. But I cannot.

For the most part, the colonial history that I know is born of the curriculum of the former East London Model C school at which I was educated. My history lessons throughout canvassed names like Ferdinand Magellan – the Portuguese who is credited as the first man to sail around the world; Christopher Columbus – the Italian who 'discovered' America; and, of course, the Dutchman Jan van Riebeeck – the man who 'discovered' South Africa in 1652.

I was told about the French and American Revolutions. From Napoleon Bonaparte to Otto von Bismarck, I was told of World Wars. From Adolf Hitler to Benito Mussolini, I was told of the Allied Powers of Franklin D Roosevelt, Winston Churchill and Joseph Stalin.

They loved to tell me about Idi Amin, and vilified Robert Mugabe.

They scantily brushed over Kwame Nkrumah, Mwalimu Nyerere, Jomo Kenyatta and Kenneth Kaunda. They could not avoid telling me about Rolihlahla Mandela, Mangaliso Sobukhwe and Mahatma Gandhi.

They drummed in William Shakespeare, Charles Dickens, Rudyard Kipling and William Wordsworth. AC Jordan, SEK Mqhayi, DM Jongilanga, TJ Jabavu and WB Rubusana were swept under the carpet. I have just learnt of Nat Nakasa. I had to read *Animal Farm* but not *Ityala lamawele.*

Sadly, I was not taught of the Punic wars between what is now Tunisia (then Carthage) and the Roman Empire, when Senator Cato declared, '*ceterum censeo delendam esse Carthaginem*' – 'besides which, my opinion is that Carthage must be destroyed'. I was not told about the Battle of Isandlwana. The Bulhoek Massacre is not known to me. I was not told of the slave trade.

I was not told about the battle of the oldest tertiary institute title that is actually contested between the Moroccan and Egyptian universities of Al Quaraouiyine and Al-Azhar respectively. I was not told who founded mathematics. It is as if the manuscripts of Timbuktu never were.

They never told me how Bantu Biko died. I was not allowed to lament the tragic story of Nongqawuse. They kept silent about Sarah Baartman. They did not celebrate Tiyo Soga. Little has been said of Charlotte Maxeke.

Nomzamo Madikizela-Mandela is a villain and 'did not deserve him'. How dare they? I was not taught about Thomas Sankarra and Haile Selassie.

They did not tell me that Sudan was the first Afrikan state to be independent, but am told of it as a failed Afrikan state.

De Klerk advocated for apartheid. Today he defends it. Yet, somehow, he received the Nobel Peace Prize standing next to his prisoner.

I was not allowed to grieve the Land Act, the Separate Amenities Act, the Group Areas Act. Rather, I must celebrate the Constitution. And how I do!

Why would they tell me these things, though? They sat at a dinner table with carving knives and produced the Treaty of Berlin. They brought with them 'civilisation' and took gold, platinum and diamonds. They also forced our strongest, youngest, most fertile and fittest across the Atlantic. For good measure, they occupied the coastal land and lapped up the sun – vastly different from the snow.

Considering I have so little knowledge of what I should know, and so much of what I do not necessarily need to know, I cannot claim to be learned, even though I have a senior degree at law.

There cannot be another generation of this direction-less drift.

Never, never and never again!

White supremacy vs transformation

SIPHOKUHLE MATHE

A university is a microcosm, a space that amplifies a country's macro-politics easily. Much like the rest of South Africa, the University of Cape Town (UCT) is struggling to effect transformation. Whereas we cannot deny the many policy changes that have already been made to address the injustices of the past and move towards greater equality, apartheid's systemic legacy lives on. This is preventing UCT, and other public institutions, from realising the Constitution's ideals.

Over the years, UCT's admissions policy has attracted much attention – in particular, the debate about race as an admission criterion. The new admissions policy seeks to use race as one of several criteria to determine whether a prospective student can be classified as previously disadvantaged. This acknowledges that black people's experiences are not homogeneous – and that some individuals, like me, had the privilege of attending former Model C schools, affording us a better-quality education that allowed for easier university access. In this regard, the university understands how class and race often intersect.

The new admissions policy aims to assess prospective students' backgrounds. Apart from race, it considers the qualifications of students' parents, reasoning that this speaks to the cultural and educational capital that parents may have imparted to their children – capital that could further advance their children's educational agency.

However, I find this criterion problematic. It assumes merit as its operating principle, and that a person's advancement should depend on his or her intellectual ability. Whereas this philosophy has value, other factors need to be taken into account, too. For one, merit cannot stand without agency. A child may be bright, but his or her agency will depend on how his or her talents have been honed and whether he or she has learnt to fulfil the requirements of his or her educational system. Merit depends on agency, and vice versa.

Then, while the university relies partly on the National Senior Certificate (NSC), this is not the only factor that decides whether a student will gain entry. It also uses the National Benchmark Test to determine the prospective student's linguistic and mathematical aptitude.

The problem with this system is twofold. Firstly, the education system in its current form does not prepare learners for university adequately. Secondly, the National

Benchmark Test is a means by which the university can sift through applications and reject prospective students whose NSC results qualify them for admission.

The question is whether such a system is truly transformative and helps to change the racial demographics of a mostly white university. The students most affected by the National Benchmark Test system are black students: students who attend good private and public schools perform better in this test. What this comes down to is a system that favours white students from former Model C schools – a system that entrenches white supremacy and does not represent a true commitment to transformation.

Another factor that should be taken into account in this regard is that the institution's donors are mostly white. For as long is this is the case, white interests will take priority to ensure continued funding; the institution does not get full funding from the government.

South Africa's per capita spending on education is among the highest in the world, at 20 per cent of the government's budgeted expenditure (R254 billion for 2014/15). However, problems with the availability and dispersal of student funding persist – problems that affect mainly black students who often have to turn to bursaries and scholarships (awarded on merit) and the National Student Funding Aid Scheme (NSFAS), for which one qualifies based on conditions of entry and financial need.

Students need to pay back a portion of the NSFAS funds

they receive once they start working. Consequently, students arrive at university for an education and leave with debt. Private stakeholders assist where they can, but help from all sectors of the economy is important. The burden of poor black students is that once they leave university, they have a responsibility to provide for their families – not usually expected of their middle-class and white counterparts.

I have been disgruntled, lately, because of a certain denialism among white South Africans.

I have had one too many conversations about race in which white people find it necessary to claim that not all white people are racist. They also claim that they are not the beneficiaries of apartheid, and that Broad-based Black Economic Empowerment (BBBEE) is making it difficult for them to get jobs.

They deny that white supremacy is entrenched. They lean on white-owned, propagandist media to draw conclusions about the state of the nation. And they speak of freedom, and of Nelson Mandela. They often pick up on my anger and call me a racist.

The denial of white privilege is hegemonic. I have learnt, over the years, about the convenience of the privilege that allows for this denialism. For instance, as a man I can deny my dominance over women because I can speak duplicitously in my personal capacity – but not in relation to the patriarchal system, which favours me systemically. Likewise, white people can claim that not all white people are racist in their personal capacity, only to evade talking in public about the system that guarantees their dominance.

Privilege allows you to skirt the issues while the pain of the marginalised demands to be felt.

I went on a lunch date with a white friend a while ago, and expressed how aggrieved I was about race relations at the university and in Cape Town. He told me that I must 'work hard and make a success of my life'. My success, I explained, would depend on how I related to whiteness. If I remained complacent about white supremacy, I would likely become successful – because of my agency, the very agency that the average black person does not have and which I obtained from my education, a product of white supremacy.

The lesson I drew from this conversation was that white people have an ignorant view of racism. To them, racism refers only to personal acts of racial discrimination. This, of course, is a myopic definition of racism. It ignores the fact that racism is structural and that personal acts of discrimination are merely sanctioned by institutional culture. The reality is that a confrontation of this structural privilege leads to deflections that suggest black people's destitution as being a result of their laziness or unspoken sub-humanity. There seems to be no interest from white people to relinquish the privilege they think they have earned.

Another thing I despise is the use of Nelson Mandela's name in debates about race. I have immense respect for the things he did, but there was a time when I could not reconcile myself with some of the compromises that were made on his watch. My anger was misguided, however – I should have directed it at those who use his name to sabotage true transformation.

It irks me when white people see the flames of black people's anger, then use Mandela's ideas about peace and reconciliation to extinguish them. Firstly, this anger has value. Secondly, how can we talk about reconciliation if the system still entrenches white supremacy? Reconciliation Day should be scrapped as a public holiday until such a time as the majority of black people feel that reformist policies are starting to translate into equitable justice. It is false to live as if we have arrived at the Constitution's destination.

The University of Cape Town is often described as the world's best Afrocentric university, which is true in only one sense: the university is in Africa. The principles on which the university operates and how it acts as an institution are clearly Eurocentric.

Several physical symbols on the university's Upper Campus depict the defeat of black people. Until recently, for instance, students were greeted by the statue of the imperialist Cecil John Rhodes, whose wealth was built on the back of enslaved black labour. As one proceeds into the Oppenheimer Library, one sees a sculpture of a naked Sarah Baartman, a monument to the hypersexualisation of black bodies, the ridiculing of black people and the exploitation of blackness. Leaving the library for the food court, one is confronted by another piece of art: a huge animal with a black man in its stomach, speaking of the defeat of the black man and his consumption by white supremacy, capitalism and other oppressive systems.

The expectations that the university has of its students and academic staff, and the research being done there, are also Eurocentric. The university remains untransformed even on the level of the professoriate. Associate Professor Xolela Mangcu has broken the silence about the challenges that black lecturers face. Not one black woman has a full professorship at UCT – most of the academic staff are white, and a professorship depends on acknowledgement by colleagues within your field of research. If your academic ideas are not in line with those of your white colleagues, how do you convince them of the merit of your work? UCT is a white academic space that celebrates the ideas of white academics.

The university's curricula are Eurocentric, too. It offers only one course that teaches students the language for articulating their discomfort in patriarchal, white spaces:

a second-year Sociology course on race, class and gender. I did not register for that course, but was a regular guest in the class. I could reflect, there, on my life through a sociological lens, which made me realise that not all hope was lost. This same sociological lens will help me to further the black feminist cause with which I identify.

However, we should not despair: UCT is on the brink of a transformative revolution, the kind of revolution in which members of the university community, especially black students and staff, will not let the university's management determine the transformation agenda's terms.

We should note, too, that transformation at the university is not just about race politics. The transformation agenda should also encompass issues of class, gender, sexuality and disability that are relevant to the workers, the students, the professoriate, the administrative staff and other members of the broader UCT community.

Democracy is coming to life again. The deferred South African dream will not produce yet another promising document, but a holding to account of the university at every turn. I believe that the momentum of this movement will inspire the rest of the country and put an end to South Africa's white liberalist post-apartheid regime.

Re-dreaming Africa

SIMPHIWE DANA

I wonder: is there a link between language, cultural identity and innovation?

According to the Department of Linguistics of the Norwegian University of Science and Technology, language is 'a granary, a repository of the world-view of its speakers, it is this particular language that best contains and expresses the indigenous belief systems of any society. New belief systems are immediately related to these existing systems. Then it goes without saying that a successful conceptualization and implementation of the societal transformation that is development can only be achieved through the use of the mother-tongues or the languages indigenous to the society.'

Or, as the academic and writer Ali Mazrui put it: 'Can any country take off if it relies on foreign languages for its discourse on development and transformation?'

The philosopher MSC Okolo has this to say about the

importance of language: 'The most virulent element working against the repackaging of the African personality is the vision of Africa in colonial languages. Of all human inventions, language alone affects, structures, defines, interprets all other aspects of human life. Beliefs, ideas, ideologies, culture, knowledge, experience, values, prejudice are acquired and conveyed through language.'

And sociologist and anthropologist Kwesi Kwaa Prah contends that '[n]o society in the world has developed in a sustained and democratic fashion on the basis of a borrowed colonial language. Underdeveloped Africa remains so partly on the account of cultural alienation structured in the context of the use of colonial languages.'

These authors seem to believe there is a link. Frankly, so do I.

Western culture has always had a superiority complex. If you do not conform to its definition of intelligence, it deems you inferior. This has seen Western culture coming to play a paternal role in the world and being responsible for cultural genocide in Africa and elsewhere.

Colonialism curtailed Africa's development, bringing with it – and enforcing – new concepts about being. It also brought new knowledge systems that were at odds with African ones. This is not to say that Africa should have rejected all foreign knowledge. However, I believe that Africa should have rejected the wholesale replacement of indigenous cultures; that said, it is difficult to say no with a gun to your head.

'Civilising' Africa was many a colonial power's excuse as they raped and plundered the continent, building their monuments and leaving broken societies in their wake. To kill a tree, you must cut out its roots; if you cut off only its branches, it will grow anew come springtime. To kill a society, you must disassociate its members from what informs their world view – their culture, language and identity. With nothing of their own, they become willing slaves to your agenda. If you take only their land and leave their societal fibre – their knowledge systems – intact, they will soon come back into themselves.

Exploring Africa, the online portal of Michigan State University's African Studies Center, describes a world view as a system of values, attitudes and beliefs that give people a mechanism for understanding the world and its everyday occurrences. Perhaps we should think of a world view as a language. Can you imagine how hard it would be to explain or understand everyday occurrences without the right words for doing so?

Words help to shape the way we see, and therefore explain, events. Similarly, the world view – the values, attitudes, beliefs – to which an individual is exposed from birth influences how she understands everything that happens to her, her community and her world.

Sadly, most African countries that gained independence

before South Africa have not fared very well, because they have not done away with colonial culture and knowledge systems. By the latter, I mean systems of governance, education, language and religion. African countries have internalised colonialism's inferiority complex to such a degree that they fear breaking away from it.

Can we blame Africa for not trusting her own intelligence? Psychologists say that if you've been abused for long enough, you start to internalise the hate that comes with the abuse. You start to believe it is for your own good, and may even start to see your abuser as saving you from yourself. But you cannot run from yourself forever.

African countries are crumbling one by one because they have sought to sustain colonial systems instead of re-dreaming Africa. Their systems are failing because the knowledge systems on which they are based are foreign to the African landscape. Thus, the African cannot use them to innovate.

South Africa was the last African country to gain independence, albeit a compromised one. We are the richest country in Africa not because the previously disadvantaged have made great strides towards economic emancipation, but because of the compromises made during our transition to democracy. These compromises more or less maintained the apartheid status quo; the impact of BBBEE can be described as the crumbs of a huge pie, accessible to an elite few.

Furthermore, those in whom we put our faith to lead us back to ourselves after independence were so far gone in their own pursuit of colonial excellence that they could pay only lip service to African identity and innovation. It should come as no surprise that the Western Cape is the country's best-run province, even as it marginalises Africans, Coloureds and Indians – the system best serves those who know how to work it. This in no way makes the African incapable; sadly, everyone – including the African – believes it does.

In this regard, we should also consider the issue of education in South Africa. Year after year, the education crisis deepens. Yes, we understand that despite the huge education budget, there are still not enough resources to equip the under-resourced black schools that apartheid has disadvantaged. We understand that curriculum changes, poorly implemented, have destroyed learner and teacher morale.

But here is an interesting fact. Between 1953 and 1976, the apartheid government phased in mother-tongue education, which improved the matric pass rate significantly. Its abolition led to the Soweto uprising in 1976; thereafter, the pass rate dropped to as low as 44 per cent.

I believe the introduction of mother-tongue education could drastically improve learner performance. Having complex concepts explained to you in a language that you understand – one based on your world view – gives you a distinct advantage. The only ones in our education system today with an advantage are descendants of colonial culture, or those who have adopted it. This further entrenches inferiority and superiority complexes.

How can one describe the African world view?

I believe that when Steve Bantu Biko spoke of Africa giving the world a more human face, he was referring to the African's harmonious, spiritual understanding of the world and his or her interaction with it, the reverence for nature, and the social cohesiveness of the Ubuntu philosophy. But to give a human face to the world, Africa must first rediscover her own humanity. Biko spoke of this at length: how the aggressive dehumanisation that black people had suffered had to be met with an equally aggressive rehumanisation to infuse life back into their empty husks.

What is this self-love of which he spoke? Is it not the love of what makes an African human? What informs the humanity of an African? Is it not her world view, her knowledge systems, her spirituality? Would it not, then, be fair to say that the emancipation of the African starts with her embracing her own – indigenous – knowledge systems and world view?

If a language is the repository of its speakers' world view, let South Africans speak an African language. If development is seen as the sustainable socio-cultural, economic and technological transformation of society, let

South Africa do business in an African language. Since no society in the world has developed sustainably and democratically with a borrowed colonial language, let South Africans be taught in an African language.

I believe that any African language carries the world view of all African ethnic groups. Our world view has given birth to our knowledge systems and our culture; to strengthen them is to fast-track development.

We have a wealth of information we are not tapping into. Africa is a rich continent, yet its inhabitants are poor – because they want to import, instead of export, knowledge and innovation. This is a sure path to neo-colonialism: this time, we will have only ourselves to blame if opportunists pillage our continent again.

For it to have any real impact on our overall evolution, education in Africa must ultimately be viewed in this way. It must teach African excellence in languages that convey the world view from which thousands of years' worth of knowledge has stemmed.

We may not know why we are here on earth, or why we have developed in such diverse ways. We are, however, finding increasingly that our cultural uniqueness has given us knowledge that others do not have. We all need to contribute to the global information pool. The question is, what can Africa contribute to the world?

Defining ourselves

SENTLETSE DIAKANYO

African culture is what defines Africans and distinguishes them from different cultures. Sadly, though, colonial rule altered African culture, religion and traditional practices significantly.

Intruders into Africa felt an unsolicited and desperate need to 'modernise' Africans and indoctrinate them to accept a European way of living, thinking and worshipping. The reason for this was their view of Africans as largely primitive. Even today, some regard Eurocentrism as a measure of social advancement and modernity. Conversely, African values and principles are frowned upon.

Neglect and deliberate suppression by colonial hooligans gradually impoverished African cultures. Fortunately, the rise of African nationalism heralded campaigns by Africans to guard against external influences on their way of life.

We need to draw a clear distinction between culture

and tradition, two concepts that are interconnected but not the same. Culture primarily refers to the value system and shared attitudes that characterise a group of people or society, their human expression and the way in which they perceive and interpret the nature of the world around them. It is what defines society, which is why a dilution of culture implies a loss of identity and uniqueness.

African cultural practices have a particular meaning that speaks to the values we embrace as Africans. While the content of culture as projected through certain practices should never change or be compromised, the tradition through which cultural meaning or values finds expression does evolve.

Tradition is fluid. It ensures continuity of culture and its transmission from one generation to the next. Africans fully understand what informs their traditional practices, and know what the meaning and relevance of such practices are. With each generation, traditional practices that have become archaic or irrelevant are usually abandoned.

As a practical example, the cultural practice of paying lobola is a traditional custom that aims to unite two families. It is intended as an expression of gratitude by the groom-to-be's parents to the bride-to-be's parents for having presented them with a wonderful and beautiful future daughter-in-law. At the same time, it is a way for the groom-to-be to communicate to his future parents-in-law that he is capable of supporting of their daughter.

Traditional lobola payment took the form of cattle – before the emergence of paper and plastic money, cattle were the primary source of wealth. However, the dictates of modern times have rendered cattle largely irrelevant as a form of payment. So African families who have embraced social advancements accept cash. Despite this change to traditional practice over successive generations, lobola's cultural significance remains unchanged.

African culture is reflected in music, food, art, language and jewellery, among other things. These are the distinguishing features of the world's different cultures. They are what make us who we are and identify us as belonging to a certain culture. Often, those on the outside of a culture do not understand the meaning or origin of these features.

The most contentious question, of course, is who can claim to call themselves African?

I say black people are Africans. Africans are black people. The term African refers predominantly to a racial identity and goes beyond the sentimental claim that being born in a certain geographical location – somewhere on the African continent – makes you African.

If you are not black and you embrace African culture, it may afford you a sense of belonging to African society, especially if you live on the continent. But it does not change your racial identity as a person of European descent, for example. White people who are born and bred in Africa claim to have roots on the continent. However, belonging by an accident of birth does not make one an African in its true sense.

The claim that we are all Africans because Africa is the cradle of humankind is also absurd: people in the rest of the world do not refer to themselves as Africans.

Africans have, in the past, over-extended and compromised themselves in the pursuit of harmonious coexistence. Africans in South Africa have walked the extra mile since 1994 to extend a hand of reconciliation – a hand that the historical offenders, who should be at the forefront of efforts to forge unity and reconciliation with those they have wronged, have frequently shunned.

Non-Africans have long had a dismissive attitude towards Africans who are unapologetic about who they are and what being African means. Some feel threatened by African nationalism, and see collective African pride, perhaps, as a threat to their privilege.

Africans need to reclaim their identity, religion and culture and discard practices that have been imposed on them. The glaring difference between the culture of Africans and pseudo-Africans lies in the former's Afrocentricism and the latter's Eurocentricism. One cannot claim lineage with Africans when what defines you is not rooted in Africa. Africans embrace Afrocentricism, as popularised by former president Thabo Mbeki, as the central element of the African renaissance.

As Africans, we cannot allow our identity to become

dispensable in the name of social expediency. The colonial era reduced African identity almost to nothing. Having liberated themselves from this historical thuggery and asserted their identity, Africans should take care, today, not to be blackmailed into watering down what defines them and who they are for the sake of inclusivity.

Africans must reclaim and defend their identity, lest we revert to the colonial days when defining ourselves was the task of others.

The post-apartheid colony: Rhodes must fall

SIPHOKUHLE MATHE

It took the bravery of Chumani Maxwele, a black male student, to throw excrement at a statue donated to the University of Cape Town (UCT) to commemorate the legacy of Cecil John Rhodes – imperialist, slave trader and white man whose legacy South African history books celebrate even as they erase his criminal activities. It was a turning point: the passivity of black pain had found a language, a voice and, more importantly, the defiance to challenge UCT's institutional racism.

I remember seeing Maxwele standing next to the statue, educating passers-by about white arrogance at the university. The stench of excrement reached Upper Campus. When a friend and I passed him as we rushed off in the direction of Middle Campus, it did not occur to us that he had vandalised a statue and that there would be consequences. I certainly did not believe that very much would happen – before his tenure as SRC president, Ramabina

Mahapa had written about the representation of institutional racism through the university's symbols, architecture and artwork, but the university had not responded to any of the memoranda calling for a review of these symbols.

The university declared the act of throwing excrement inappropriate, and further asserted that there were more peaceful ways of protesting that did not involve vandalism. Furthermore, the university charged Maxwele, arguing that letting such acts go without consequence would set a precedent.

The SRC responded promptly, citing solidarity with aggrieved students for whom Maxwele's sentiments resonated. This was significant: it mobilised students to question the university's modus operandi on issues of transformation. Momentum built, student support became protest action, and the SRC finally had a voice, which was to become the Rhodes Must Fall (RMF) movement.

The movement increased support as it lobbied for all stakeholders, such as maintenance staff, the professoriate and teaching staff, to find a voice. One of its first demands was for Vice Chancellor Max Price to commit to a date on which the statue would fall. The symbolism of this call, it was argued, was that it assessed the university's seriousness about heeding the call for transformation and tested the extent to which the gesture would be the starting point of meaningful engagement.

The engagement, however, was to be on the students' terms, actively challenging the system that had seen management determine the terms of engagement before. This position would be attributed to the movement's revolutionary nature – it aligned itself with Biko's assertion that black people should oppose 'the intellectual arrogance of white people that makes them believe that white leadership is a sine qua non in this country and that whites are the divinely appointed pace-setters of progress'. This, of course, was met with the 'metaphysical guilt' of whiteness that accounted for Max Price's excessive defensiveness, which often granted more respect to due process than the voices and pleas of the black students who had had enough of bureaucratic traps.

Part of disrupting white arrogance at the university was the occupation of the Bremner administration building, the offices of the university executive. This occupation demonstrated students' impatience with management about the removal of the Rhodes statue. Claiming black space allowed students of the movement to reimagine the university as Afrocentric, embodied in their renaming the building 'Azania House' during their occupation.

In this reimagination of UCT, the demand to remove the statue was merely a precursor. The language changed: no longer was 'transformation' the term for post-colonial reimagination. Instead, the term 'decolonisation' took centre stage, citing the need for students to unlearn the

European values that had been imposed on them and that had alienated them from an institution that should have come to represent the richness of African culture.

The curricula that obsessed about European philosophy and culture faced interrogation, too. Curriculum was earmarked as a site for decolonisation, with black students commenting that they could not find themselves in their curricula, despite their being hammered – ironically – with the idea that their UCT education would teach them to find African solutions to African problems. This exposed the dislocation of African politics, displaying Europe's economic and social transportation to Africa and how colonialism's transcendental nature needed a microscopic review at the university.

Politics within the professoriate centred on white men's domination of the academy. This dominance meant that the peer reviews of black and women researchers' work were met with contempt at times, to the extent that black and women lecturers had a harder time being recognised as full professors. The university had always maintained that it would not employ too many black academics at the expense of competence. The racism of this assertion came to the fore, exposing the fact that employing black academics was not synonymous with compromising meritocracy as white arrogance would suggest.

Regarding maintenance staff, the university's outsourcing policy meant that UCT contracted companies that employed the workers who were based on the campus. So maintenance staff at UCT did not enjoy UCT benefits such as medical aid and housing allowances. The more pressing implication of this is that it shifts accountability from the university to the companies that it employs, be it the Jammie Shuttle or Super Clean. In the event of maintenance staff, G4S security staff or Jammie Shuttle drivers having worker-related grievances, UCT would turn them away: they may work on campus, but are not university employees.

Other issues included policies about changing contracts and tender processes for outsourced companies. If UCT were to contract a new security or cleaning company, the new company would be obliged to grant the workers on campus the choice to be employed by the new company. The movement's main argument, however, was that UCT could simply insource workers to strengthen its account-ability to the labour force on campus. The RMF move-ment thus gave the labour force a voice, which is why a NEHAWU workers' march and other events carried momentum for all discerning voices on campus.

Contrary to popular belief among UCT alumni and the white Zionist community, RMF was not a populist move-ment that tried to compromise the university's governa-bility. The movement simply wanted to disrupt white, supremacist, patriarchal, heteronormative ableism. In its disruption of the Bremner building – or, rather, Azania

House – it hosted many events and seminars that gave members of the movement the language with which to articulate the campus experience. The movement, as I expressed in Panashe Chigumadzi's research for the Ruth Fellowship award, gave intellectual 'self-defence' classes to marginalised people on campus.

During the Azania House occupation, the likes of Xolela Mangcu offered a great deal of political education, sharing their experiences as Black Consciousness scholars and black academics at white liberalist universities. Other prominent figures, such as Achille Mbembe and Pumla Gqola, were invited to offer their discourse and were excited about what was unfolding at the university.

Inevitably, the politics of the movement became nuanced, with race issues taking centre stage. Though the movement claimed to have an intersectional approach to issues of transformation at the university, there was an over-emphasis on race – perhaps because the language for speaking about racism was far more advanced and accessible than the language for speaking about gender inequality, for example. The dominance of black men saw black women in the movement claiming that the space was equally theirs, and that the idea that revolutionary militancy lay in the hands of black men needed to be subverted. After all, only humanity needed recognition. This raised questions about the legitimacy of what was claimed to be an intersectional space.

The need to uphold intersectional politics resulted in a resolution: the movement's men would either just listen or be absent when women were given the platform to discuss their issues. These men would also assemble separately to think about ways in which they could dismantle patriarchy. Likewise, white allies would assemble separately when black people were given the space to express themselves. The guiding principle of this was to allow a true sense of freedom among oppressed people.

The movement claimed that people could speak *of* other marginalised groups but not *for* them. At times, black middle-class student leaders would speak *for* poor students, *for* workers and *for* queer people, but not *of* them. At other times, black men would speak *for* women, deny patriarchal male privilege, and claim racism against black people as the main oppression, failing to recognise patriarchy as a system of oppression as a result. Feminists of the movement brought literature and feminist thought to the fore, exposing how difficult it can be to acknowledge privilege and demonstrating that black men need to understand that their hypermasculinities needed as rigorous an interrogation as white supremacy if the revolution were to remain intersectional.

The replication of apartheid protest theatrics was noteworthy in this post-apartheid revolutionary movement, which begs the question whether the negotiated settlement really destroyed systems of oppression. Protesters shouted 'One settler, one bullet', and raised symbolic PAC hands and ANC struggle fists. White people's anticipated discomfort led to the 'one settler, one bullet' slogan being reported to the Human Rights Commission. Many white people felt that it constituted incitement to violence, but the movement countered that it was not advocating white genocide but the end of white supremacy and the dominance of the intellectually arrogant 'settler minority' that Steve Biko spoke about. The message was that the revolution did not aim to ensure the comfort of the privileged – all it sought to do was to disrupt white supremacy and its long-standing protection.

Many myths were put to bed, including some about the experiences of middle-class black students and their construction as Model-C-schooled 'coconuts'. The movement revealed the myth that these students were immune to black experience, whatever blackness is, by virtue of their closer assimilation into whiteness and a culture that either tokenises them as ambassadors of whiteness or treats them with all the contempt of white supremacy. As something of a middle-class 'coconut' myself, my identifying with the movement received responses such as, 'I had had so much respect for you, Sipho. I can't believe you go in for all this stuff about us white people being racist. I am really disappointed in you.'

Undoubtedly, this was because I'd attended a largely white high school. My politics, whether Pan-Africanist or liberalist, had not had much of a voice there – particularly because the high-school environment had always been falsely regarded as an apolitical one. My pro-black politics, about which I was now more vocal, lost respectability, primarily because they were no longer aligned with the 'peaceful' and 'non-racial' Mandela politics that white people use to arrest real engagement with decolonisation and transformation. The RMF movement thus created a space for students who had lived with racism in white institutions prior to university to interrogate blackness in a predominantly white space. This opened the eyes of those who had been unaware, and refined the understanding of those who had been aware but who had had no voice.

At UCT, the era of consciousness has persisted. RMF was a prelude to events such as the Zizipho Pae saga. Pae, a religious fundamentalist and former SRC vice president, described the legalisation of same-sex marriages in the United States as 'institutionalising sin'. The result of this violent sentiment about the rights of LGBTIAQ+ people was what came to be known as the Queer Revolution, which regarded Pae's statement as hate speech and intolerance about queer bodies. During this saga, some students were on vacation. Curiously, RMF did not show solidarity at the Queer Revolution's protest march and subsequent press conference – yet another incident in which RMF's intersectionality came to question. It exposed, yet again, an over-emphasis on the racial struggle and the dire position of queer people in this struggle. It also exposed the RMF movement's heteronormative dominance.

The Queer Revolution was a moment of cognitive dissonance for black queer people, who felt that despite their support of RMF's racial struggle, few supported their Queer Revolution. Sentiments arose that RMF was dominated by selfish, hypermasculine black men who would fight for their own liberation, but not for that of queer people. Was the RMF movement's intersectionality mere window-dressing, aimed at hijacking votes and support? Was it political opportunism on the part of black males? As I raise these questions, I become fearful: as a black man, I want neither to detract from RMF's objectives nor to give RMF's critics ammunition to delegitimise it. I do, however, believe that the movement is worthy of fair criticism at every turn, and that there can be no silence in response to pertinent questions like these.

The political arena for student activism is fertile, with RMF extending beyond UCT's borders to the rising movements of #OpenStellenbosch at Stellenbosch University, the Black Students' Movement at Rhodes University, and other universities facing white racism and arrogance. All of these student movements represent determination to end the culture of white liberalism – that is, the culture of white liberals setting the pace of transformation.

By extension, the movements agree with Achille Mbembe, who decries democracy as having suspended revolution in South Africa.

RMF and other student movements should be lessons for the ANC. The white liberalism that the ruling party represents and protects is the very thing that will determine, in the long run, how sustainable the party's power really is. Black Consciousness is relocating itself in the post-apartheid colony. Black is finding new definitions in the realm of race, class, gender and disability.

Black is rising. Azania is rising.

5

Comic relief

Life lessons learnt from taking the taxi

YOLISA QUNTA

I'm fully aware that Hollywood's sole reason for existence is to sell us (unattainable) dreams, but I often find myself falling for them. Take, for instance, how taxis are depicted in movies. These gleaming yellow contraptions seem to ferry only good-looking types around New York (yes, always New York); generally, only one person occupies the taxi – two at most.

Because of a sad series of events that left me without a car, I was forced to take public transport. Within days, my ideas about New York taxis were shattered forever.

In South Africa, of course, the word 'taxi' means something completely different. Our taxis are minibuses built to transport a minimum of 16 people, but they usually transport anything from 20 to 25 passengers. They also gleam, mostly – likely because of the multiple layers of touch-up paint that are meant to cover innumerable dents from chasing up and down our roads like drivers from hell.

Allow me to share the following truths I have learnt about South African taxis:

1. Your personal what?

Forget the images of passengers reclining luxuriously in the back seat while gazing raptly at the bright lights of Times Square. Your reality will most likely be multiple strangers seated practically on top of you.

Taxi drivers have a healthy contempt for namby-pamby concepts such as personal space, and an equally brazen disregard for what the laws of physics dictate about how many human bodies can be squeezed into a limited amount of space, All you can do is hope, fervently, that your fellow passengers are well versed in the basics of personal hygiene.

2. He who holds the money, holds the power

Unless the driver has a *gaardjie* – a person who collects the fares and usually offers running commentary on everything from traffic to passengers – one of the passengers will be designated to collect all the money. Until every single penny of that money is accounted for, nobody is safe.

Your entire commute can be held up for 45 minutes because the driver is five bob short. Oh, and don't try to hurry things along by offering to donate the missing money. This is deeply offensive to the driver's pride – most revel in their reputations as tough, no-nonsense characters. It may also cast the suspicion that you are the culprit.

3. Disco nights

Whether you are in a brightly painted, souped-up taxi with a sound system whose bass dissolves your insides gently, or an *ekasi* taxi blasting *mbaqanga*, there are no limits to the genres of music to which you will be exposed. Take a ride in to town to learn more about the latest local and overseas hits, or simply about the driver's favourites.

Because the taxi is his mobile kingdom, the driver holds sway over the sound system. As supreme overlord of the vehicle, he also gets to choose which type of music to play and at what volume – usually one that will destroy your eardrums and definitely any hope of having a normal conversation with a fellow passenger. Passengers who try to object are immediately given the option of disembarking minus their fare.

But it's not only the taxi driver with whom you have to contend. In the era of smartphones having turned everyone into virtual DJs, you are also subjected to the playlist of the brethren next to you for the duration of the journey. Before the advent of MP3s, I thought that being subjected to strangers' conversations was bad enough. Now my eardrums are tortured on the daily commute. I suspect my fellow passengers might be deaf, because I can hear every single tune from their headphones as it competes with the taxi's tunes.

4. Let the stickers guide you

In a number of taxis, you'll find stickers intended to inform and entertain you and, occasionally, to give insight into deep philosophical questions. They are short and to the point. Personally, I find them very amusing. If nothing else, they help you to avoid eye contact with undesirables and educate you about taxi etiquette.

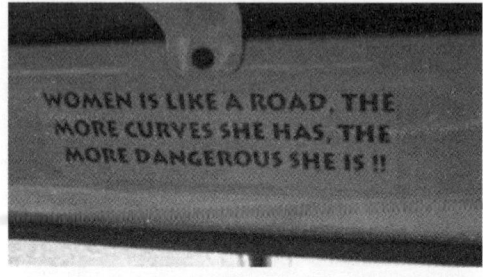

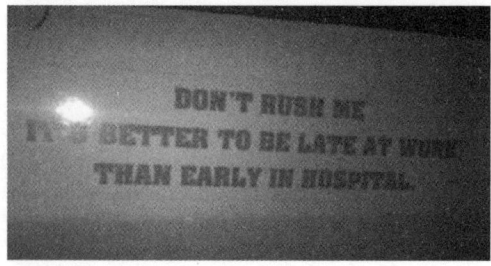

Photo credit: Yolisa Qunta

5. Taxi Ubuntu

Taxi passengers usually take the concept of community very seriously. This means that, for the duration of the trip, your fellow commuters will make your business their business.

The earnest-looking person in the back seat will judge you harshly when you tell him that you haven't accepted Jesus into your heart, don't want to buy Herbalife, and are not interested in being hooked up with his nephew or in joining his stokvel.

Expect them to comment on how you did not run fast enough when the taxi stopped five kilometres away from where you were standing. Should you need to phone some-one, the person sitting next to you will eavesdrop openly on your conversation.

If you think of taxi rides as an extreme form of boot camp that compresses all the life lessons you ever needed into one crowded, sweaty, loud ride, you could emerge from the experience a better person. Where else can you perfect your accounting skills, get up close and personal with strangers, dodge unsolicited advice and get a whirlwind tour of contemporary music all in one go?

Think of it as a temporary and unglamorous phase that will pass more quickly than you can imagine. One day you, too, will be whizzing past behind the wheel of your own car or be driven by a suited chauffeur – or possibly even skip traffic altogether and take the yacht.

Uber may be all the rage these days, but life in a taxi will always be more fun.

Why are you asking me these questions?

Q&A WITH DAVID KAU BY
YOLISA QUNTA

David Kau first popped into the public eye doing a series of hilarious TV commercials for the Toyota Tazz. Before that, the comedian had been quietly honing his craft on stand-up stages around the country. He produces and stars in the showcase *Blacks Only*, currently in its tenth year. I hoped I could use our friendship as leverage in persuading him to add one more thing to his busy schedule.

. . . which didn't work out as I'd anticipated. Firstly, persuading David to write took numerous phone calls, text messages, and some not-so-subtle tweets and e-mails. In other words, I went into low-key stalker mode. He then claimed that he was not really a writer, that producing stand-up content wasn't the same as writing. In the end, we compromised; I agreed on an interview.

After another telephone relay, I nailed down a time. Midway through our interview came his question: 'Why are you asking me these questions?'

Here are the results.

Yolisa: What is your most vivid memory of growing up in apartheid South Africa?

David: The first time I experienced teargas. I was seven years old, and in Standard 1. That would be 1985. There were riots, and it was quite a distance between home and school, and there was no public transport available – buses and taxis were getting stoned and petrol-bombed. I was with older people I didn't even really know. Along the way, they were looting local shops. At least they gave me a sip of their Coca-Cola.

Yolisa: Tell me about the biggest differences for you personally post '94.

David: The biggest difference post '94 is having the freedom to live – to live where you want to or can afford to, to work or study in the field that you want to be in, and to be with or marry the people you want to, regardless of race. Freedom to travel anywhere in the country, and in the world.

Yolisa: As a comedian, do you have any limits? Are there jokes you won't do because they are too controversial?

David: The only jokes I won't do are jokes about rape. Other than that, comedy has to do with timing, and it is a business. You pay me. I make you laugh, sometimes make fun of you. I'm not trying to be controversial, but if there's something controversial about my jokes, then – Whoop! – there it is.

Yolisa: Do you get tired of people asking when PMS is coming back?

David: No, I don't get tired of it, but I do wish they understood and accepted that it isn't. It's been eleven years now, and there's more to do in life, and in comedy, and in the world.

Yolisa: You have performed in plenty of other countries. How do you compare South Africans' sense of humour to that of other nations?

David: South Africa has way more freedom – or, rather, the comedians have much more freedom – compared to other countries. Most comedians I have worked with, especially from the UK and USA, find they have a lot more things they can say when they're here in South Africa than when they're where they're from. Other countries are still more conservative.

The only thing in South Africa that sometimes becomes tricky is culture, or the differences between the many black cultures we have. A simple thing like a greeting makes a difference to an African audience. Greeting them in their mother tongue or in English, or knowing someone's clan name or your own, all make a difference in how your show or performance begins and how they welcome or don't welcome you, which tells you if they're going to laugh or not.

Yolisa: Do you even get mistaken for someone famous?

David: Yes, some people still call me Dadaman from *The*

Phat Joe Show. Lately, I take a lot of pictures as David Tlale. I never say no . . .

Yolisa: You started off doing purely stand-up but now you have diversified into production, online media, motivational speaking, etc. Tell me how this process happened?

David: Kagiso Lediga and I had always wanted to make movies. We came up with the idea for PMS when we were second-year UCT (1997), and we only fell into comedy in 1998. I guess everything took on a life of its own. Comedy took first preference because we made it look so easy. It paid a lot of money, it involved just you and the audience, no cast or writers or directors or business partners. Then there came a time when we knew we were capable of doing more, and we mostly only ever worked at night and not a lot, so we had a shit load of time on our hands. At least, I did.

Yolisa: What's the most random thing you've ever been tweeted by one of your fans?

David: 'My aunt/grandmother died pls tell me a joke.' This was just weird and awkward. A bit psycho, too. Sometimes you just have to move on and read the next tweet or delete and block. Twitter is not real life, so I treat it exactly like what it is – a social media app, which is one of hundreds.

Yolisa: Would you recommend stand-up as a career choice?

David: It's not really a career choice. It's more of a calling.

It can't be taught, but once you have it, it can be refined, packaged and sold really well.

Yolisa: What do you think South Africa will look like in 20 years?

David: I hope we have flying cars and shit. If we still have squatter camps, then they must come in, like, a small box that you can just press a button and your little squatter room appears. Basically, I hope we have high-speed internet and are not still behind Kenya. I hope there's less corruption, not zero corruption. As long as people's lives are better.

No more load shedding. I'd also like my family in Kroonstad not to have to buy water like they do now, because the water coming out of the taps is dirty or undrinkable. Less crime would be a win–win.

More jobs, more tourists and, from the way things are looking right now with the era of 'yellow bones', I'm sure there will be more Coloured people – or mixed people, as they prefer to be called. Hopefully South Africa will not have a white president; it will be too soon.

I digress

LOYISO GOLA

It was only fairly recently that our president admitted that he was, indeed, responsible for some of the costs of the upgrades at Nkandla. For so long, he'd insisted that he owed the state nothing for the improvements at Nkandla, since they were all security requirements.

When I heard about the Nkandla scandal the first time, I couldn't help thinking about the reality TV show *Extreme Makeover*. In this show, the host, Ty Pennington, pays a visit to an unsuspecting family (usually of 10), listens to their sad story, and then packs the whole family off on a vacation before proceeding to renovate their house in the few days for which they are on holiday. On the family's return from sunbathing in Hawaii (Americans *love* Hawaii), they are welcomed into their newly made-over home.

Let me tell you about Ty Pennington: he can turn a four-roomed apartheid house in the township into Narnia (I wonder if Narnia also has service delivery protests?).

I could picture Zuma coming home from two weeks at, say, the World Economic Forum in Davos to the recently renovated Nkandla. He would be especially thankful that Ty stuck to the black, green and gold theme. He probably thought to himself, *How did the man know my wife needed a tuck shop? He even added a bunker and an AstroTurf soccer pitch . . . wow!*

I have often wondered why the apartheid government built toilets for black people outside their houses. As a child, going for a pee after an episode of *Velaphi* late at night was the scariest mission, and the talk of witchcraft did not help to inhibit a child's imagination. Growing up, for me that was the worst thing about apartheid – that and having to learn Afrikaans.

Sorry, I digress. Back to the president. The president strikes me as a person who is on top of things (well, with that many kids, he is top on something). I wonder if he's fathomed that he is in charge of the biggest economy in Africa – I remember how he once stated at a press conference that he was not aware of the details about what happens in every department.

Mr President, I realise that you don't know exactly what is happening on a daily basis in all state departments, but when you are speaking at a press conference, at least make me feel like you are in control.

This is the penalty of leadership. Why do we fire coaches instead of the players? The answer is simple: because coaches are the leaders of the team.

A president, a CEO, a manager, or any other leader who admits that he or she was not in control of a particular situation will diminish the confidence that underlings have in him or her. Such a leader will sink with the ship.

We all know presidents have people who write speeches for them. This is no secret. Yet, at the State of the Nation address, we don't say 'the president's speech writer said', we say 'the president said'.

Why doesn't the president do the State of the Nation address in Zulu? Just a thought.

Sorry, I digress.

That's how we toyi-toyi

Q&A WITH SIVUYILE NGESI BY
YOLISA QUNTA

I like to think I'm a person who learns from her mistakes.

When Sivuyile told me he was not a writer but was happy to be interviewed, I believed him the first time. Siv Ngesi is an actor, stand-up comedian and owner of a magnificent set of abs that he shares regularly on social media.

Here he is in his own words.

Yolisa: What is your earliest memory of realising that you were different from other people?

Sivuyile: Growing up, I used to wonder if white people had the same colour shit as we do. I was about five years old when I had this thought, and at this point I realised there was a difference.

Also, my mom didn't beat around the bush about anything. She used to say white people don't wash and that they smelled. All black parents used to say that. They would say, '*Hamba uyohlamba, uwungumlungu.*' You can really translate that!

Yolisa: As a youngster, did you have a lot of interaction with white people?

Sivuyile: Yes, and that's possibly why I get into trouble so often, especially on Black Twitter. I was raised in such mixed worlds and consequently, I'm not biased and I know right from wrong. I don't care what colour you are, wrong is wrong and I'm quite blunt about it. But if I get in trouble for the right things I don't give a fuck.

Yolisa: You have done two stand-up shows called *Race Card* and *Dekaf.* What do your audiences look like, and do audience members react differently to your jokes according to their race?

Sivuyile: I live in Cape Town, so the demographics are fairly white. There isn't much of a culture of African people going to the theatre unless they are out to see the David Kaus and Loyiso Golas of this world.

Because of my upbringing in different environments, I think I create a very comfortable environment for different people. The odd person gets offended, but then again, if no one gets offended then I'm not doing my job right.

Many people who get offended want their money back. I say voetsek, I've bought airtime, it's gone.

Yolisa: Is there any subject that you don't joke about because it would be crossing the line?

Sivuyile: It's not what you say, it's how you say it. There is an art to saying things. I've grown up getting away with murder anyway, and I've taken that to the stage. As Joey Rasdien said the other day, 'You know, Siv Ngesi is a cunt onstage, but in real life he's exactly the same and we love him for that. He's truthful and he won't talk behind your back. Everything he has to say he'll say in front of you.' And that's my persona.

Yolisa: Incidents of racism at establishments in Cape Town seem to be rife. Does your celebrity protect you from this?

Sivuyile: The bouncers at one of these establishments once said to me, you are fine, you're on TV. So my black is not as black because I'm on television. Going to such an establishment is a problem – we shouldn't support them.

We should all line up outside and when we get in we should all buy water. Tap water, *qha*. That's how we toyi-toyi. There is a problem here, but we are not re-solving it correctly from our side as Africans because we continue going to these places. That's not helping.

Yolisa: So, you think the way forward is a boycott?

Sivuyile: Completely! They should not make money off us. It's like they are a gigantic light attracting us moths because they play 'our music' and we love that music but they don't really want us. How does that work?

Yolisa: Race is such an integral part of South Africa but

we seem unable to engage about it properly. Do you think it will always be like this?

Sivuyile: The thing about human beings is we've made up an imaginary friend in the sky who died on the cross for us. Human beings always need to be led and have someone control them. That's how we are programmed. There must be someone above us, or someone we are oppressing.

When it comes to different races, one group always needs to be above another. Growing up, as black people we considered Coloureds below us. They in turn thought they were better than us, but our parents told us they were beneath us. That's just how human beings are. The only way it will stop is when we all start having sex and bringing out Coloureds. Then we will all look the same.

Yolisa: You think that's the only solution?

Sivuyile: Absolutely. I have friends who live in Poland who have no idea what racism is. In very white places, where there are no black people, they don't know what it is to look down on another race.

Yolisa: Isn't it odd that we are still experiencing this problem twenty years into democracy, especially since we are the majority?

Sivuyile: It happened in the beginning when they first came to Africa. We were, like, come, let's share. That's the kind of mentality we have as African people. Then they came, took advantage of us and it's been downhill ever since.

6

Thinking beyond privilege

Cape Town's pretend partnership

ILHAM RAWOOT

Very few situations in my life have made me want to throw up. One of these happened on a certain evening in March 2014; the impulse lasted for nearly three hours. That night, the Cape Town Partnership (CTP) presented a 'debate' about how to include Cape Town's citizens in projects related to the World Design Capital campaign.

According to the World Design Capital website, the campaign is an international, biennial, city-promotion project. It highlights the accomplishments of cities that have used design as a tool for improving social, structural and economic life. That year, Cape Town had been chosen.

I was excited: here was an opportunity to engage constructively on this controversial topic with people at the top level of the Cape Town Partnership, a non-profit (Section 21) organisation that aimed to 'mobilise and align public, private and social resources towards the urban regeneration of Cape Town's central city'.

The invitation, which I received via e-mail, said the debate would be about including people 'from all walks of life' in World Design Capital projects. The debate was held at the Assembly, which is a club on most other nights. I wasn't sure what exactly the invitation meant by 'all walks of life', but I had a feeling the bouncer outside the Assembly was there to decide.

As I entered the venue, I was struck with confusion. Barring about fifteen of the 250 guests, everyone was white. Where was the rest of Cape Town? Granted, most of them live out of the city centre on the Cape Flats and in the northern suburbs, but words like 'ordinary people' and 'active citizens' in the invitation had led me to believe that they, too, would have been informed about the event and that transport would have been organised.

I was lucky enough to meet the project manager, Caroline Jordan, at the bar, where I was redeeming my soft-drink voucher.

'How was the event marketed?' I asked.

'On social media – Twitter and Facebook – and via e-mail,' Caroline answered.

'What about the people in Delft who don't have Twitter and e-mail?'

'My maid has e-mail.'

'Wow.'

'What would you suggest as a solution?'

'Flyers, posters in taxis, information-sharing through

the many participants with whom you apparently engage . . .'

'Okay, we'll think of that next time.'

'Why was there no public transport?'

'We are near two transport hubs, the MyCiTi bus service and the train station.'

'Would you, as a woman, travel back to Khayelitsha on an empty train at 9 p.m.?' (Silence.) 'I didn't think so.'

This was the start of what turned out to be an unrelenting barrage of patronising, racist and exclusive sermons.

The event began with an introductory address by the Cape Town Partnership's chief executive, Bulelwa Makalima-Ngewana. The panel was made up of mostly foreign-educated Africans, the ones who intrigue white people because they are 'so well spoken'. Makalima-Ngewana is a town planner and was one of the key role players in developing Cape Town's Central City Development Strategy (CCDS) in 2008. She is clearly an intelligent woman, and appeared to have good intentions. However, while she reminded the audience that she had grown up in a township, she didn't have an answer for why there was no marketing for the event on the Cape Flats. She suggested that the relevant audience member stay behind to give her some contacts.

Makalima-Ngewana presented a video montage of 'average' Capetonians looking very happy about, and grateful for, all the city has provided for them. There were jolly beggars, most of whom had been kicked out of the city by the police. The montage also showed a group of Coloured teenagers in school uniform. Neither they nor their parents were at the event. The majority of the Coloured population lives on the Cape Flats, the area to which they were forcibly removed under the Group Areas Act. In many parts of the Cape Flats, residents face death by stray bullets every day.

This wasn't in the montage.

The teenagers were there to highlight the apparent diversity of the city and to show how the different races and classes in the city all live happily together. They were marketing ploys: there to bring some colour into the mix. Few people knew the reality of what they'd head back home to when they left the city bowl. It was difficult to listen to the inspiring rhetoric about inclusivity and accessibility – just one drum short of a rousing version of 'Kumbaya' – when a quick look around the room revealed the contrary.

During the discussion, Gavin Mageni – who heads the South African Bureau of Standards Design Institute – said that South Africans need to be more engaged in active citizenship. Mageni hails from Marikana. Whatever came out of his mouth once he'd revealed this was said in the light of this fact. Are *you* from Marikana? No? Then shut the fuck up.

He was challenged by a German academic who pointed

out that in a country that was referred to as the 'protest capital of the world', a statement about the lack of active citizenship in Cape Town was naturally problematic. He believed that strikes were a form of active citizenship, probably in its purest form, as they manifest the basic democratic rights of assembly, expression and political engagement.

'No!' said Mageni. 'Violence [read: strikes] is not the answer!' (Fist-shaking.)

Mageni believes that entrepreneurship is the one and only key to active citizenship. Striking miners and, by extension, unions are the antithesis of his value system, which is built on self-reliance and DIY citizenship. If you have to strike for your right to serve a master other than yourself, you have failed the test, in his opinion. Also, as an entrepreneur, the market is ostensibly your best friend – which is why, for him, unsettling the economy through strikes is 'selfish' and 'antisocial', because the market will provide. It does for him, at least.

Then there was the film director Sunu Gonera, who has some good credentials – he was awarded a scholarship to a private school in Zimbabwe and now makes documentaries. He went on a long stroking session about how he had made it in Los Angeles: 'One day I was talking to Clint Eastwood', 'I go up and down between here and LA', 'I have dinner with some of the best film directors in the world'.

He tells his story to 'boys at Bishops' and 'boys in Khayelitsha', because he wants to show them that if he could make it, so can they. That's motivation in theory, because it ignores the fact that most of the children in Khayelitsha will not receive scholarships, because their classroom windows are broken and their teachers don't get paid much and many of them risk being stabbed for R10 on their way to school. Most of those children will not have the opportunity to excel in the classroom.

The theme of much of the discussion was that in order to be an active citizen, South Africans needed to be self-made entrepreneurs and pull themselves up by the boot-straps. But if they're not able to, they needn't worry, because a major benefit of the Partnership's activities was job creation.

What kinds of jobs are we talking about? I wondered. Promises of jobs are irrelevant when the issue is addressed on its own – having a job does not automatically get you out of poverty. What alleviates poverty, for example, is when structural issues like the cost of housing and health care are addressed. But the upper-middle-class panel didn't care to tackle the issue in that kind of depth.

Anyway, Mageni – who looked dapper in his suit and red tie – said that if they wanted to get to where he was, 'young people need[ed] to stop having this sense of entitle-ment'. To live and be happy in their own suburbs, they should create a community they wanted to be a part of, and should not necessarily want to go somewhere else (read: into the white city centre). So, they should stay super chilled out in council flats in Heideveld and Bishop Lavis: neighbourhoods with not a blade of grass in sight, whose sons are forced into gangs, and whose daughters run the risk of rape every time they walk out the door.

That they are there for reasons of history and would likely remain there for generations to come should not be taken into account. On top of everything, they should fix the situation themselves, because they dare not have a sense of entitlement. Needless to say, this kind of conversation about entitlement is dangerous. It ignores the structural dynamics against which poor people have to struggle daily, and which prop up the middle class.

The discussion, which a friend described as a group wank, went on for two hours. This event was possibly one of the only chances the public would get to engage with the top level of the Cape Town Partnership.

After the discussion, when the panel walked off the stage to be photographed and interviewed on video, I cornered Mageni. But from the get-go he was not interested in my questions about the relevance of strikes, because he Was From Marikana and I Was Not From Marikana. The 2012 Marikana strike, it seems, is the only example of a strike in South Africa's history. As far as he was concerned, all strikes are violent, regardless of who opens fire first.

Could this be because of the lack of access to, and discussion with, top-level management and boards of mining companies? No – it was purely the trade unions' fault.

He discredited every challenge I threw his way because he had lost ten family members in Marikana and I had never been to Marikana. Actually, I said, I'd spent years working in Marikana. The non-argument ended with him shoving his finger in my face, shouting with unashamed vitriol, 'Who are *you*? Who are *you*? Who are *you* to tell me about strikes? Who are *you*?'

Then there was an awkward moment in which we both tried to descend the narrow stairs at the same time.

I left the Assembly sickened. Not only had an opportunity to engage with the city's people been wasted, but the charade had been offensive.

The Cape Town Partnership should have been more honest about its agenda – that it wanted to continue designing a more tourist-friendly European-style city while keeping the unwanted and unsightly on the other side of the mountain. The least they could have done was to pay the poor and marginalised for being cast as extras in their diversity ad.

And its execs should definitely make sure that all of their maids have e-mail.

Why I am not doing Mandela Day this year

YOLISA QUNTA

I have never made a secret of the little regard I have for the deification of Nelson Mandela, but this is not the place to go into that. What does irk me exceptionally is Mandela Day, and this 67 minutes business.

Living in a country with the highest Gini coefficient in the world, I believe strongly in giving back to those less fortunate than me. This measure of inequality shows that the gap between the rich and the poor is extremely high in South Africa. We all, therefore, have an obligation to help where we can.

Why, then, am I so uncomfortable with a campaign aimed at doing exactly that? Firstly, it bothers me that the central message of Mandela Day is that people only need to do something charitable for just over an hour once a year, and can spend the rest of the year basking in the glow of their goodness. Secondly, Mandela Day seems – increasingly – to be getting hijacked by corporates and their flashy campaigns. Mandela Day offers a host of social-media-friendly opportunities that allow even the least conscious person to do the bare minimum and then, with the applicable hashtag, to broadcast it for the world to see.

In a country like South Africa, shouldn't we all be thinking about the less fortunate every day and aiming to bring about meaningful change in our society?

A few years ago, I used to volunteer at a charity organisation called SARDA, which helps disabled children learn how to ride horses as part of their physiotherapy. As with any charity organisation, fundraising was a constant focus. Once a month, the chichi shopping centre in my fancy suburb allowed a few volunteers to shake collection tins at the shoppers. One month, one of the regulars couldn't make it. I was asked to take a 45-minute slot.

My Kanye West-sized ego balked at the thought of standing in a mall shaking a tin, asking predominantly white shoppers for money. As Olivia Pope would say, the optics didn't look good. But it was for a good cause, so I sucked it up and waded in.

On reporting for duty, I was given a tin and a roll of stickers. It wasn't as bad as I thought: time passed fairly quickly and most people were polite. Then, as I was about to start the countdown to the end of my shift, I was approached by a homeless man whose face I recognised – he hung around the mall. He greeted me and asked what I was doing.

I explained about the charity and the advantages of physiotherapy. He looked me straight in the eye and said, 'So, you're with the horses?'

When I said yes, he proceeded to dig through his many layers of clothing. After a long time, a lone five-rand coin emerged, which he carefully placed into the slot of my tin. He let me know it was because he had always liked horses. After accepting a sticker, he shambled off.

It's a good thing he left, because I did not have words to express the gratitude I felt.

While I was being childish in my angst about looking like a beggar, here came a man – who did not even have the basics that most of us take for granted, such as a roof over our heads – who was willing to give what little he had to a worthy cause.

So, every year when Mandela Day rolls around, I can only look at all the cool kids on #67minutes acting like they care and shake my head. I find them all wanting.

Mind your language
SIBUSISO TSHABALALA

One day, a year or two ago, I was amazed to hear on the radio that the Tower of Babel had grown a foot taller. At the top of the tower stood Jacob Zumu's younger brother, Michael, who – during the broadcast – had sloppily admitted to negotiating a contract for Thabo Ntshiqa, head honcho of Khumbula Property Services.

Like a half-baked court scene from *Boston Legal* or *Judge Judy* – but without a pushy lawyer or a dazed jury – for some, the admission was a thing of beauty.

'So, you put in a good word with the Free State premier in order to get a contract, is that right?' asked John Robbie.

Zuma Jr's response was a muttered, 'Yah, some would say it is that one.'

At that point, it was clear that Robbie had an unfair advantage. Like many South Africans, English is not Zuma Jr's home language. So the burlesque continued.

'And in return, you were going to get cash and you were

going to get the homestead built for you by the company, is that right?' asks Robbie.

'Yes, they made it for me. They never give me cash on the hand, but they made it for me,' replied a by then flustered Zuma Jr.

This was neither skilful cross-examining by Robbie nor top-class journalism. Michael Zuma's grasp of the English language is basic, which makes him an easy target. He is unable to offer a woolly defence or put a spin on things, as his brother's spokesperson so often does.

I did not doubt the veracity of the claims; it is probable that Michael Zuma's admission is not far from the truth. What interested me was how his admission was solicited. If public broadcasting is meant to provide news and impartial analysis, its subjects ought to be treated fairly, regardless of their background and proficiency in the English language.

If public broadcasters exist to edify, and not to confirm biases and deeply held views on issues, Robbie failed. Put differently, if Robbie's sole intention was to 'get to the bottom of this', he would have handled his encounter with Zuma differently. As a shrewd public commentator, Robbie should have been discerning enough to realise that his interlocutor was not well versed in English. He could have given Zuma more of an opportunity to state his case without being led. There's always room for rigour – but asking an inarticulate man leading questions is unfair.

The final straw was when Robbie asked, 'But you used your name, you used your contacts to help them get the contract. Even though the company had a bad track record?'

To which Michael Zuma responded: '[Dramatic pause] Hmm, pardon?'

Robbie was not alone. A few days later, the popular investigative journalism programme *Carte Blanche* also gave Michael Zuma a call. Same script, different interrogator.

Broadcasting regulations are silent on how language can be used as a tool to marginalise and even obliquely discriminate against people. My favourite South Africanism is that old chestnut about 'unity in diversity' and how we acknowledge it with our eleven official languages. Why, then, does public commentary and news only count when it is in English? There is no place, here, for funny-sounding natives who aren't articulate in the language of the Queen. Michael Zuma should not have agreed to field questions in a language with which he is not entirely comfortable, but he did.

Soon afterwards, a far more articulate and wealthier dude was caught invoking the myth of the bogeyman when he said, 'If you don't vote, the boers will come back to power.' None of the media houses that reported on it cared to tell us the language in which Cyril Ramaphosa made this comment. The ANC deputy president was addressing the residents of Seshego, Julius Malema's back yard. An educated guess would be that he was probably speaking Sepedi.

Now, the term 'boer(s)' has multiple meanings. *Maburu* or *amabhulu* is what racist white South Africans were referred to during apartheid (the terms are still used today). More significantly, the term *maburu* or *amabhulu* is a synecdoche – a literary device used to describe the system of apartheid as a whole, complete with its actors.

Again, the nuances of the word were lost on the South African media; Solidarity and the Freedom Front Plus cried racism the moment they heard about it.

If we are to build an active and open democracy, these kinds of prejudices will have to disappear from public discourse. Otherwise, we risk selling this discourse to the highest bidder, the dominant 'ism'. Classism, sexism, ageism and racism still contribute significantly to how views are interpreted and analysed in South Africa. Those entrusted with the responsibility of being arbiters of our commentary spaces – journalists, editors and broadcasters – ought to listen more carefully.

I shudder to think what would have happened had the popular Lesedi FM jockey Thuso Motaung asked the construction cartel boys in the news at that time fiery questions in Sesotho. I can see them wince as they tried to spin something in Sesotho, while humming 'Nkalakatha'.

Thankfully, they were spared the disgrace. In Robbie's words: 'Obviously, there's a language barrier.'

'If only they could stop fucking'

FEZISA MDIBI

Why is sex such a taboo subject for Africans? Why can't we simply tell our children the truth about it? What if we told them that sex is, in fact, for pleasure, that it is a wonderful experience shared by two people who feel something for each other, and that it's not just for purposes of reproduction? I asked a friend these questions recently.

My friend, who has been travelling in South America for about five years, replied that one of the people she met on her travels was an exasperated anthropologist who had been to a village where sex was not the big deal we make it out to be. The anthropologist felt that the adults were abusing the children by not imposing more restrictions on sex.

The story reminded me of the nomadic Wodaabe people of the Sahel in West Africa, who gather to celebrate the fantastic tradition of Guérewol – often referred to as the male pageant festival. Men beautify themselves and parade in front of the women. At this festival, it is not frowned upon for a 'love marriage' to occur. A 'love marriage' happens when a participant is 'stolen' by a woman; it can carry on for the duration of the festivities, or forever. For instance, a married man can continue with his 'love marriage' for life should he choose to, since the Wodaabe practise polygamy.

Although some African people have practised polygamy for centuries, and still do, the Bible condemns it. This made me think: we couldn't always have been this conservative about sex.

Growing up in rural Pondoland, I recall gatherings that were attended by unmarried youths in their late teens and early twenties. These gatherings were called *umphahlo*, and would be held at a specific house known to all the parents – what we now call parties, I should imagine. There would be singing the whole night; I'm told it was perfectly acceptable for those who fancied each other to feel each other up and play around without penetration. It was an accepted practice that released sexual tensions. There was also *ukusoma* in Zulu communities. How, then, did we get to the point at which the mere mention of sex is enough to have you sprinkled with holy water?

I believe the missionary influence in Africa has played a major role in how we see sex. We all know that it was the missionaries who brought in a new set of rules for the 'natives'. All their teachings were inspired by the Bible, which tells us that sex before marriage is a sin. What are we supposed to do with all this natural sexual energy?

Sex has become demonised at every level. We teach our children that they shouldn't even think about it, let alone discuss it with us as parents. We teach them that their private parts are dirty. Church ministers in Liberia have even blamed Ebola on homosexuality, describing it as 'a plague sent by God to punish sodomy in Liberia'.

The narrative of the 'diseased native' has also been drummed into our heads so much that we have come to believe it.

In her article 'From Miasma to Ebola: The History of Racist Moral Panic Over Disease', Stassa Edwards writes: '[W]ith the history of American and European panic over regulating foreign disease comes a history of regulating the perception of filth from beyond our borders, a history of policing non-white bodies that have signified some unclean toxicity [. . .] The bureaucratic annals of colonialism are filled with reports on the unsanitary conditions of life and unhygienic practices of natives.'

Edwards goes on to say that this intense focus on hygiene emerged from an old medical doctrine known as miasma. 'According to the miasma theory, illness was the direct result of the polluting emanations of filth: sewer gas, garbage fumes and stenches that permeated air and water, creating disease in the process.

'Filth, however, had many incarnations. It could be literal, or also a catch-all metaphorical designation for anything that made people uncomfortable about race, gender and sexuality. (This idea underpins phrases still in use today, for example: a "dirty whore".)'

When people are uncomfortable about race, gender or sexuality, myths start to emerge. Opinions become popular purely through mass consensus within one group of people who feel superior to another. One example of this is cooties, a fictional childhood disease that is used in the US, Canada and Australia as a rejection term and as part of an infection tag game (such as Humans vs Zombies). Often, the 'infected' person is someone who is perceived as 'different', such as being of the opposite sex, disabled or shy, or having peculiar mannerisms.

The latest dehumanisation of the African is illustrated in the Ebola construct, Edwards writes. 'Pernicious undertones lurk in these parallel representations of Ebola, metaphors that encode histories of nationalism and narratives of disease. African illness is represented as a suffering child, debased in its own disease-ridden waste; like the continent, it is infantile, dirty and primitive.

'Yet when the same disease is graphed onto the bodies of Americans and Europeans, it morphs into a heroic narrative: one of bold doctors and priests struck down, of experimental serums, of hazmat suits and the mastery of modern technology over contaminating, foreign disease.

These parallel representations work on a series of simple, historic dualisms: black and white, good and evil, CLEAN and unclean.'

According to Edwards, in Western medical discourse Africa is often depicted as 'an undivided repository of degeneration'. She writes that in comparing the representations of disease in Africa and in the West, 'you can hear the whispers of an underlying moral panic: a sense that Africa, and its bodies, are uncontainable'.

Edward's observations on the West and viruses shed light on how we perceive ourselves in terms of illness, especially Aids. It is the miasma theory that has led us to abandon all causes of death for Africans other than 'HIV-related illnesses'. Some time ago, a friend went to a dermatologist because she had an allergic rash on her face. The first thing the dermatologist asked her was whether she had been tested for HIV. When my friend insisted that she didn't want an HIV test, and only wanted her skin checked, the dermatologist told her that she had written a book about HIV and the skin and that my friend needed to buy it.

The HIV theory perpetuates the belief that the hardships, ill health and early death that many Africans experience are self-inflicted. You've heard the line before: 'If only they could stop fucking without a condom', or 'If they could just stop their polygamy'. Helen Zille clearly illustrates this attitude when she writes about Ebola:

'Another crucial lesson we should learn from affected countries is that this disease will carry on spreading as long as cultural taboos around burial customs are skirted.'

So tell me, *muntu*, how many of your dead loved ones have you touched lately while performing 'burial customs'?

This virus construct is a self-perpetuating, money-making tool. It keeps the money flowing out to the West while we continue to die from issues that existed in Africa long before HIV tests did. It systematically absolves anything and anyone of responsibility for the hundreds of years of oppression of the African that has resulted in the African being compromised psychologically, emotionally, financially and physically. It wipes out the history and effects of colonialism and civil wars that have continued to rip through Africa for the benefit of Western pharmaceutical companies.

A quick look at the world's two most populated countries shows that perhaps a sex virus might not be the biggest problem. Chinese and Indians somehow elude the labels of 'sex crazed' and 'promiscuous' label that Africans carry.

How do we explain these glaring differences between Africans who are HIV-positive and those from other races? Whether we like to admit it or not, HIV has become a 'black virus', one strongly linked to Africa. For example, a black friend who had been dating a white guy discovered, on the big night, that he was wearing two condoms. He admitted that he was scared of being infected.

In 2005, the HSRC claimed that 40.7 per cent of women in KwaZulu-Natal tested positive for HIV. A 2008 UNAIDS report claimed that 5.7 million South Africans were infected. Besides former president Thabo Mbeki, who ever asks what these tests actually test for?

In his opening address at the 13th International AIDS Conference in Durban in 2000, Mbeki said that the world's biggest killer and 'the greatest cause of ill health and suffering across the globe is listed almost at the end of International Classification of Diseases. It is given the code Z59.5 – extreme poverty.'

If we had been paying attention to statistics and where these 'HIV-related deaths' occur, we have to agree that poverty-stricken areas are frequently involved. As Mbeki asked, can we attribute all this to a single sex virus?

As Advocate Anthony Brink – whose book *Debating AZT* sparked Mbeki's questioning of the causes of Aids – put it, the American PEPFAR programme promotes and encourages 'celibacy, condoms, vaginal biocide, abortion, sterilization, caesarean surgery, AZT and Nevirapine for pregnant mothers and their babies, no breastfeeding, formula milk, amputation of male genital erogenous tissue and the dumping of billions of dollars of useless, toxic drugs in our country – for poor Africans [. . .] who, according to the "messages" in the media and on the billboards, need to be rescued from killing themselves thanks to their out of control sex lives.'

To think that our problems can be solved by abstinence alone is short-sighted, and part of the bigger problem. It's the kind of mentality that will see us continuing to ignore the real causes of ill health and death in our society, and the plight of those who go to bed hungry and live in appalling poverty.

Maid in South Africa*

HAJI MOHAMED DAWJEE

I stepped into a parallel universe the other day – a dog park filled with domestic workers and white babies. I may just as well have been in the movie *The Help*, set in the United States in the 1960s.

There were no dogs, just a community of maids with children who were not their own. It is not the fact that this collective was at a dog park that was surprising to me, but the fact that I was certain that just an hour later, residents of that same community, all white and upper-middle class, would be at that same park with their dogs. White people can walk their dogs, but not their children. *Or maybe none of the people with dogs have children*, I thought.

This scene may not be new to you, but it was to me, especially when I considered the transformation of that same park later in the day. For the sake of clarity, and to avoid a massive generalisation, let me say that this is not true of all white people. And maybe it is just more shocking and appalling to me because I grew up in a community (with domestic workers) where your parents or a family member either found the time to take you to the park (or a graveyard, in my personal experience) or not. And then when you were old enough, you made your own way there.

No one else was responsible for your playtime. Dogs did not really factor into the equation – if they were present, they just sort of went along. And then we moved to a white community of smallholdings, where white people did the same thing: took their children and dogs for walks. But I had never seen or experienced a distilled environment like this dog park before. It was new and, to be honest, a little sickening.

The argument about domestic workers having to raise other people's kids is not new in South Africa, nor has it been for a long time. I've noticed that Parkhurst in Johannesburg is buzzing, at any time of day, with domestic workers pushing babies that clearly aren't theirs in the Ferrari of prams. (The streets are also filled with any number of domestic workers walking pets that don't belong to them either.) Owners and parents are at work for the day, I assume, or seeing to pertinent social affairs, or – dare I say it – driving their dogs to the parlour.

And while we're on the topic of work, I take nothing away from the fact that the domestic worker environment provides jobs for many South Africans. But even this leads to important themes that are often labelled controversial, such as the treatment of these workers, fair pay, options for protection, and empowerment of workers who contribute to an economy and to communities. But for the purposes of this endeavour, I will focus on the community aspect, which is twofold.

It's unlikely that the domestic workers of Parkhurst convened and decided that every Friday at about 4 p.m. they would meet with their employers' children. I did not have the guts to go up to them and ask if this was the case. But my companion on the day made an important statement: that meeting in this way builds a sense of belonging. They were all there, doing the same thing, living the same experiences. It was a way for everyone to come together, at least. More than an opportunity for a few privileged children to go outside and play and, presumably, not to interfere with their parents' dog time, this was an opportunity to connect, converse and share.

I wondered how many of their employers or residents of the community have paid any attention to this. Are they okay with how all of this is panning out? I also wondered whether, if these domestic workers had not had this opportunity to get together, they would ever dare to say to their employers, 'No, Mrs X, I don't think it's cool that I have to walk your child to the park, or your dog, for that matter. It's bullshit. Do it yourself.'

It's unlikely.

I also find it highly unlikely that any domestic worker

has ever agreed to care for someone else's child so that her employer can spend more time with the dog. Does this sort of thing come with the territory? Perhaps there are those out there who enjoy this sort of thing. Maybe there are stipulations for extra pay, if and when needed. At the very least, perhaps some sort of conversation about these arrangements does take place between employer and employee prior to employment.

If it is simply assumed or expected that domestic workers will assume this responsibility, are their employers at least aware of how extremely unreasonable it is? Are any of these suburbanites even alarmed by this?

I'll concede that in many ways I'm jumping to conclusions here. Again, this is not a scene from *The Help* circa 1960. But maybe it should be. Maybe then it might spark an era of civil rights action for domestic workers in South Africa.

If there is any truth to my initial – unwarranted – assumption whatsoever, it begs asking: why can you walk your dog, but not your child?

* This piece was first published on M&G Online.

Acknowledgements

I would like to acknowledge the best editor in the world, Annie Olivier, for taking this book from one e-mail and a coffee date to the polished masterpiece it is now. As an unknown and green writer, I could not have wished for a better champion with whom to share my audacious dream, to push me when I needed it, to advocate hard for me and to do all the things it took to get us to this point. Annie, I am forever grateful to you for believing in my vision and collaborating to make it a reality.

Then, my sister wolves, the women whose love, encouragement, words of wisdom and endless chats have got me through my adult life mostly intact: Shani Dike, Elvine Bloemstein, Raquel Burghess, Viki Mangaliso, Shelley Armstrong, Kim de Beer, Tamyn Coleman, Pumie Msengana, Thando Ntoi and Carmen Sebastian. There are not enough words in this universe to express how your love has carried me through and above everything. Let us all keep marching towards our dreams.

To the men whose calm, dignity, strength and ever-ready credit cards have seen me through the highs and the lows, I salute you: Bruce Norris, Sonwabo Xala, Grant Solomons, Loyiso Maqgi, Martin Madlala, Andrew Morris and Kai Landvoigt. Thank you for always being hard enough to protect me and soft enough for me to call home.

Most of all, thank you to all the talented writers who let me harass, cajole, bully and beg them to donate their sterling voices to this project. I am humbled, and so grateful that you all believed in me enough to start this journey with me.